SIGHT

Cartoons for Eye Doctors and Their Patients

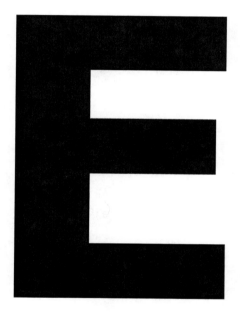

by Scott Lee, O.D.

337 Publishing
San Francisco

ISBN: 1-4196-5308-3

Published by 337 Publishing
Designed by Scott Lee, O.D.

Printed in the United States of America

For my parents, who bestowed upon me
the intelligence to become an optometrist, but
have no idea where I got the artistic ability.
And for my wife, Chrystine, who offered countless
ideas for the book, one of which I actually used.

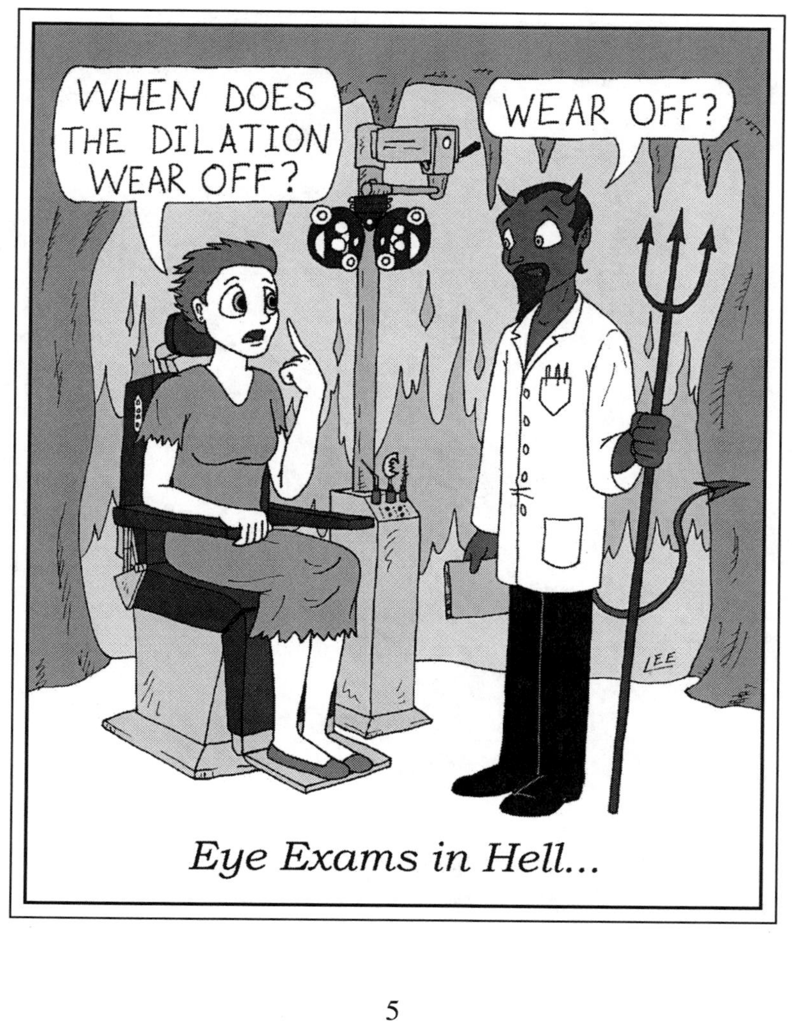
WHEN DOES THE DILATION WEAR OFF?
WEAR OFF?
LEE

Eye Exams in Hell...

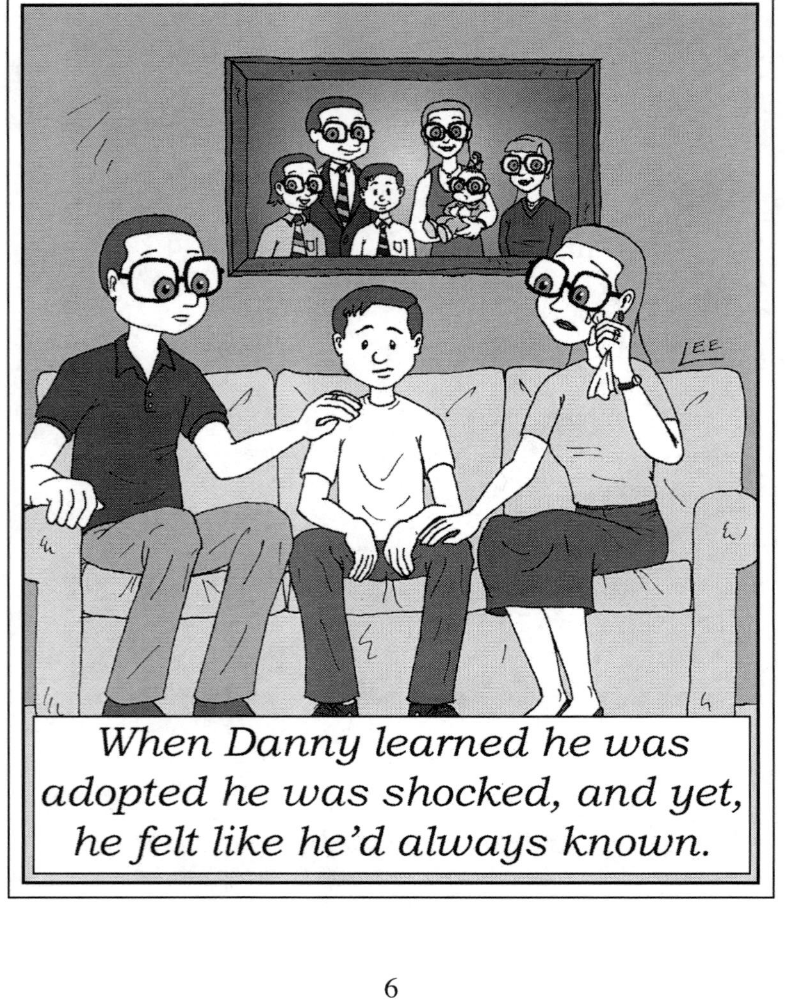
LEE

When Danny learned he was adopted he was shocked, and yet, he felt like he'd always known.

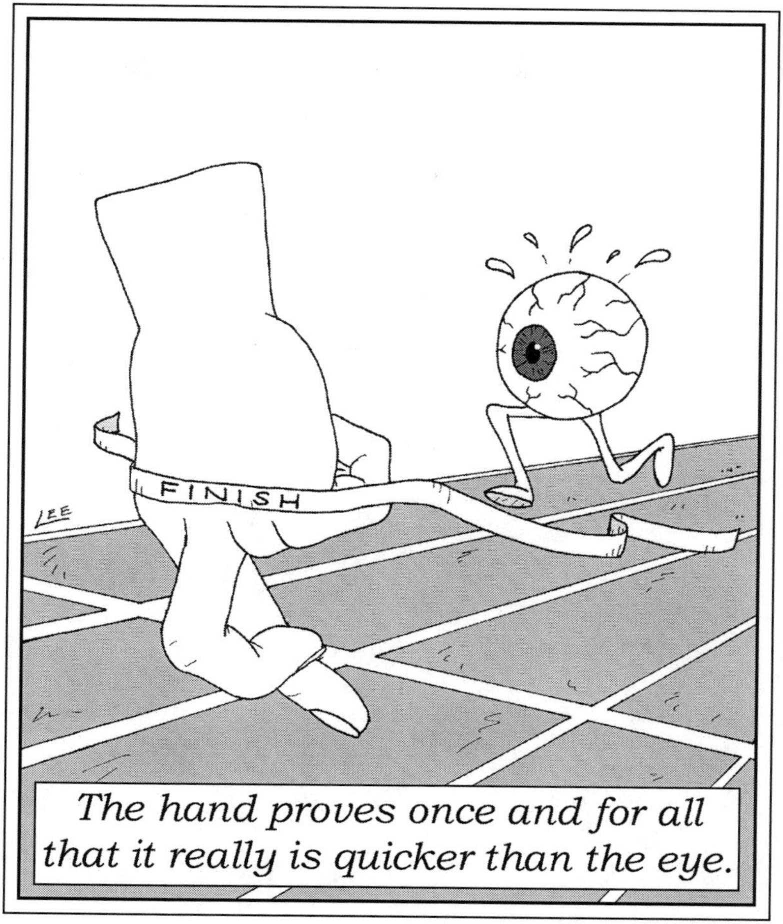
LEE
FINISH

The hand proves once and for all that it really is quicker than the eye.

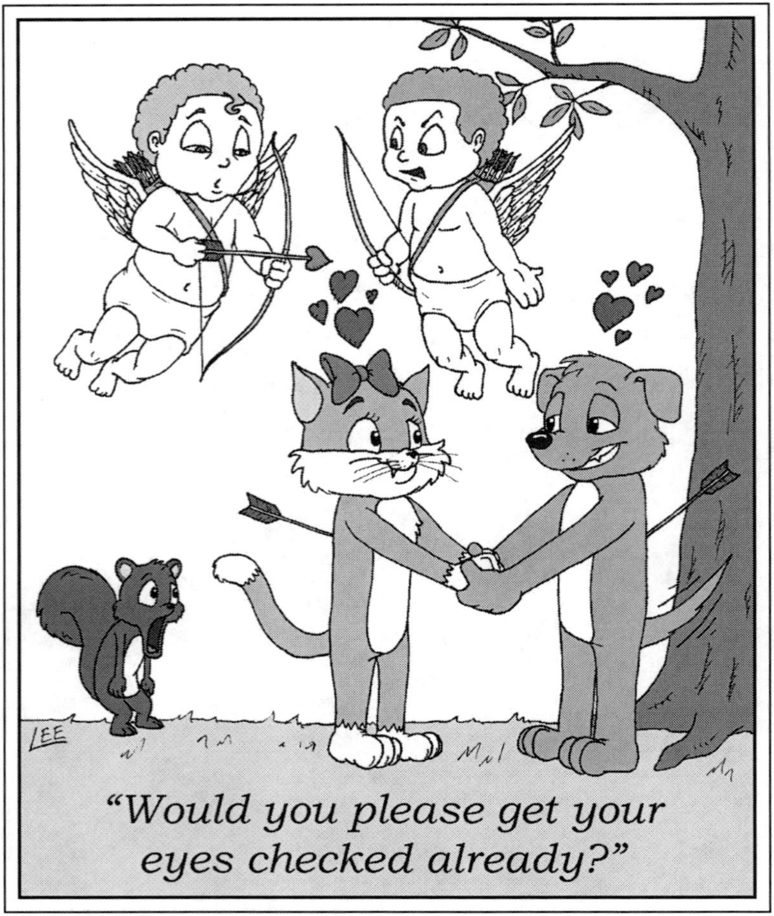
LEE

"Would you please get your eyes checked already?"

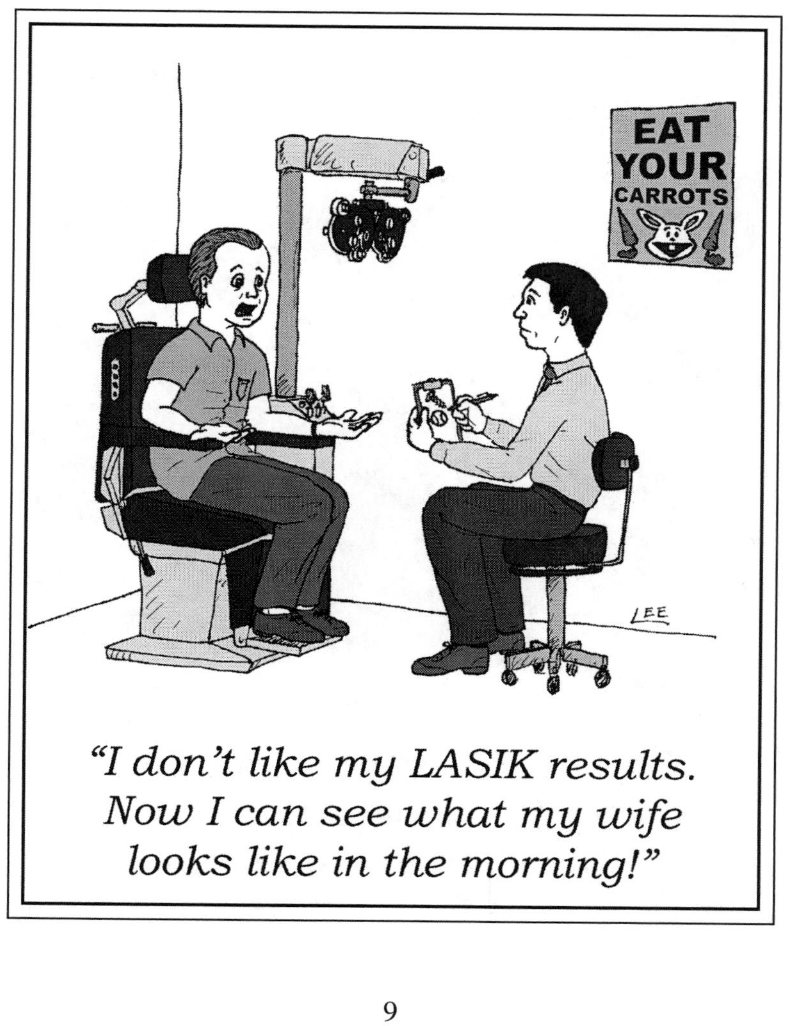
EAT
YOUR
CARROTS
LEE

"I don't like my LASIK results. Now I can see what my wife looks like in the morning!"

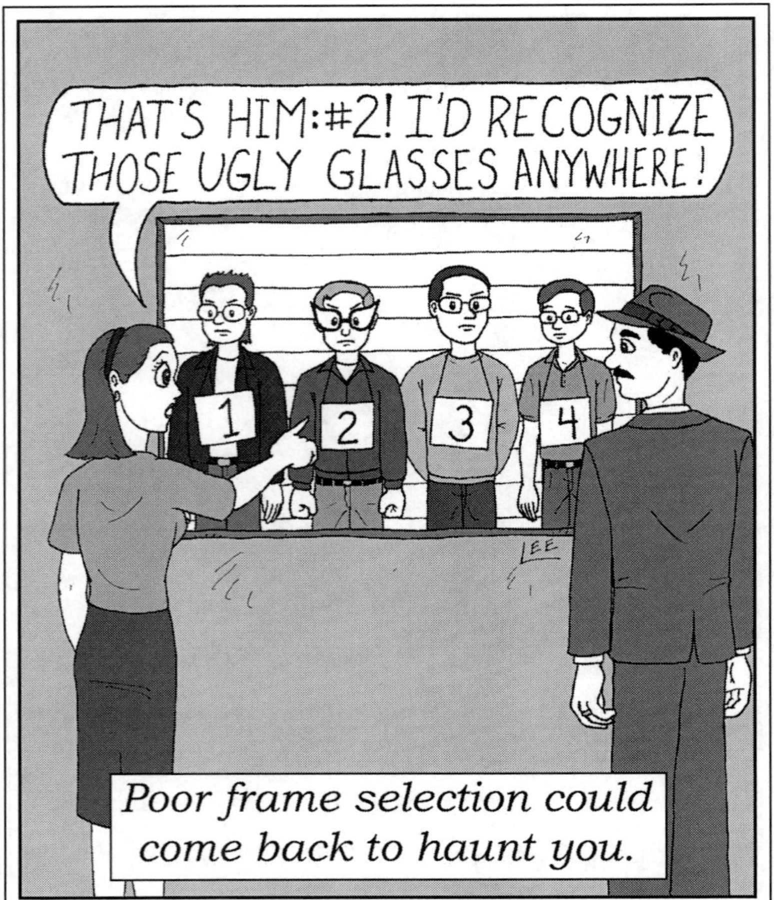
THAT'S HIM: #2! I'D RECOGNIZE THOSE UGLY GLASSES ANYWHERE!
1
2
3
4
LEE
Poor frame selection could come back to haunt you.

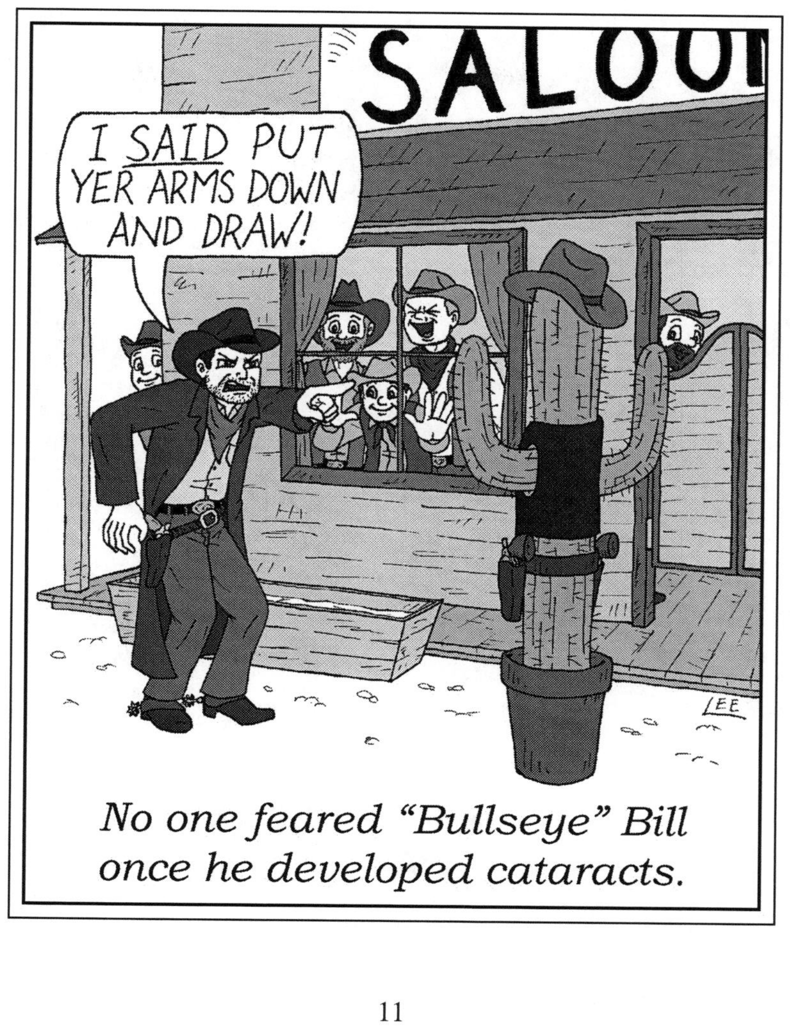
SALOON
I SAID PUT YER ARMS DOWN AND DRAW!
LEE

No one feared "Bullseye" Bill once he developed cataracts.

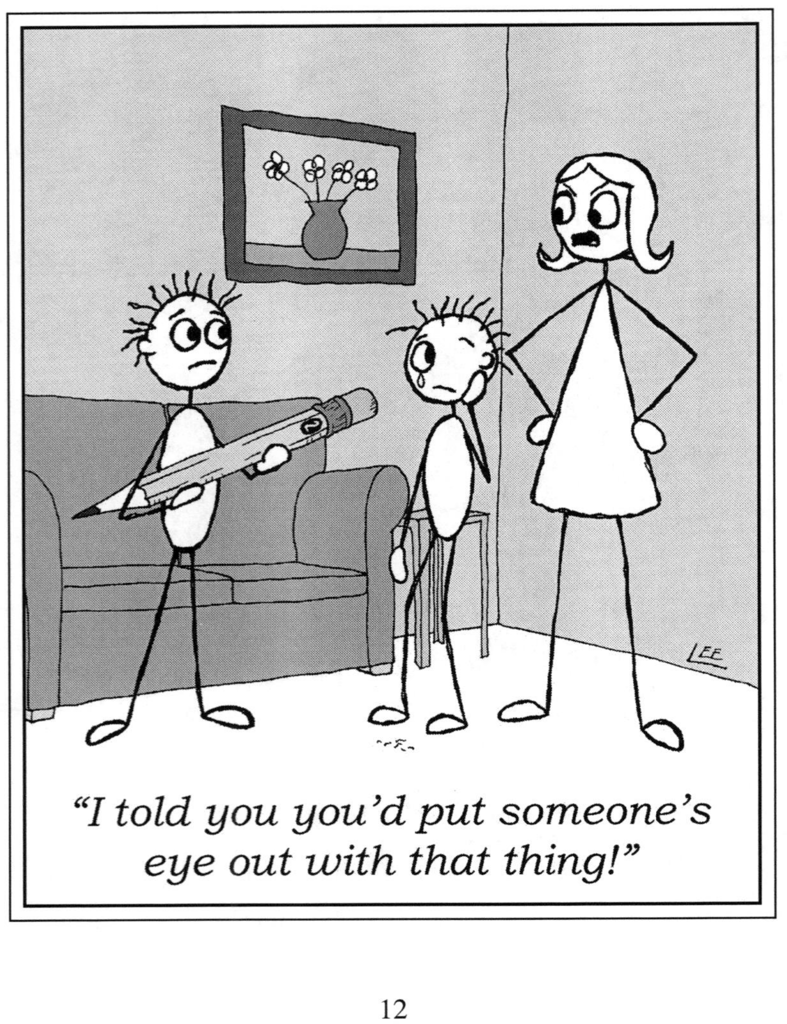
LEE

"I told you you'd put someone's eye out with that thing!"

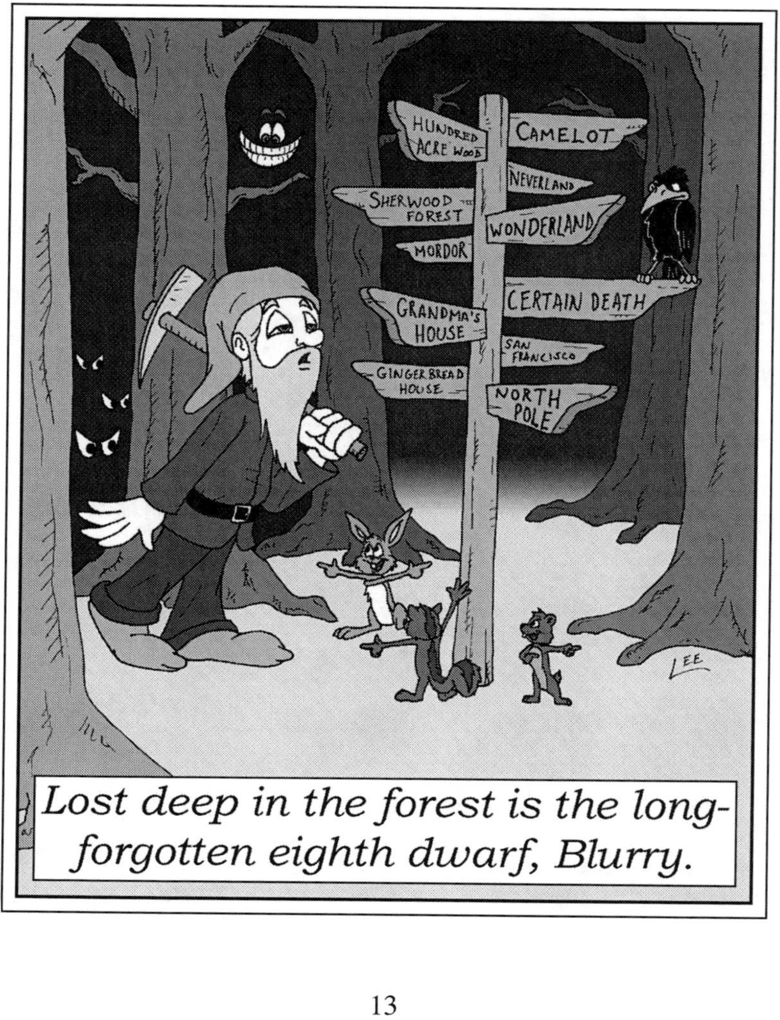
HUNDRED ACRE WOOD
CAMELOT
NEVERLAND
SHERWOOD FOREST
WONDERLAND
MORDOR
GRANDMA'S HOUSE
CERTAIN DEATH
SAN FRANCISCO
GINGERBREAD HOUSE
NORTH POLE
LEE

Lost deep in the forest is the long-forgotten eighth dwarf, Blurry.

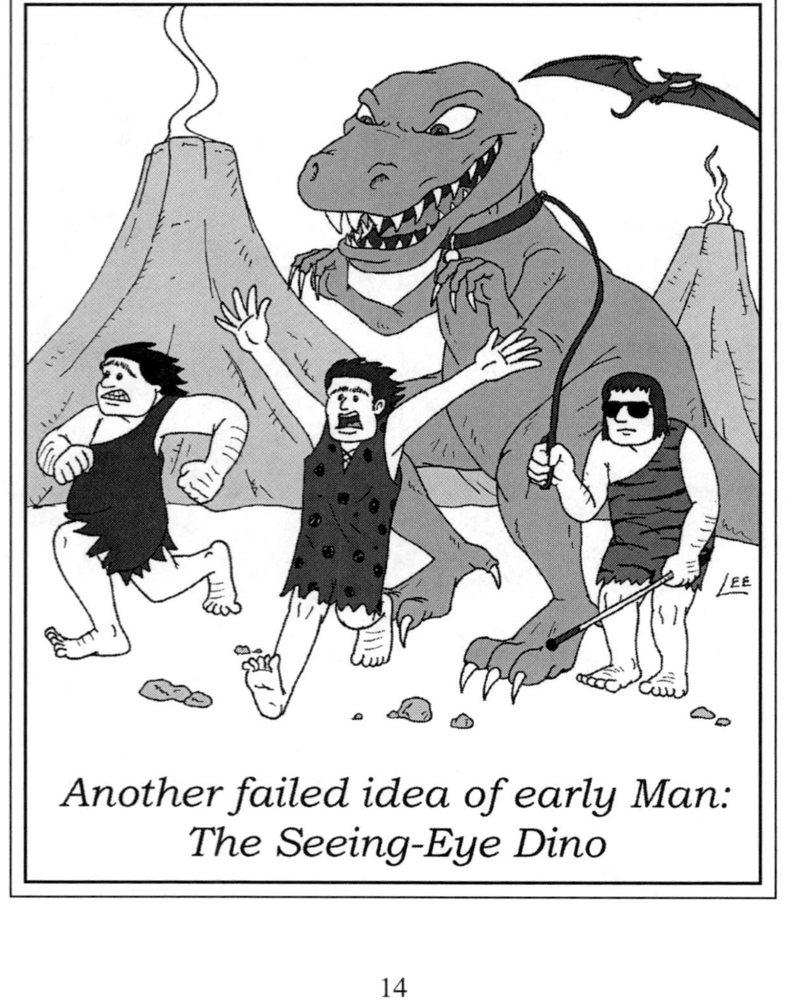
LEE

Another failed idea of early Man:
The Seeing-Eye Dino

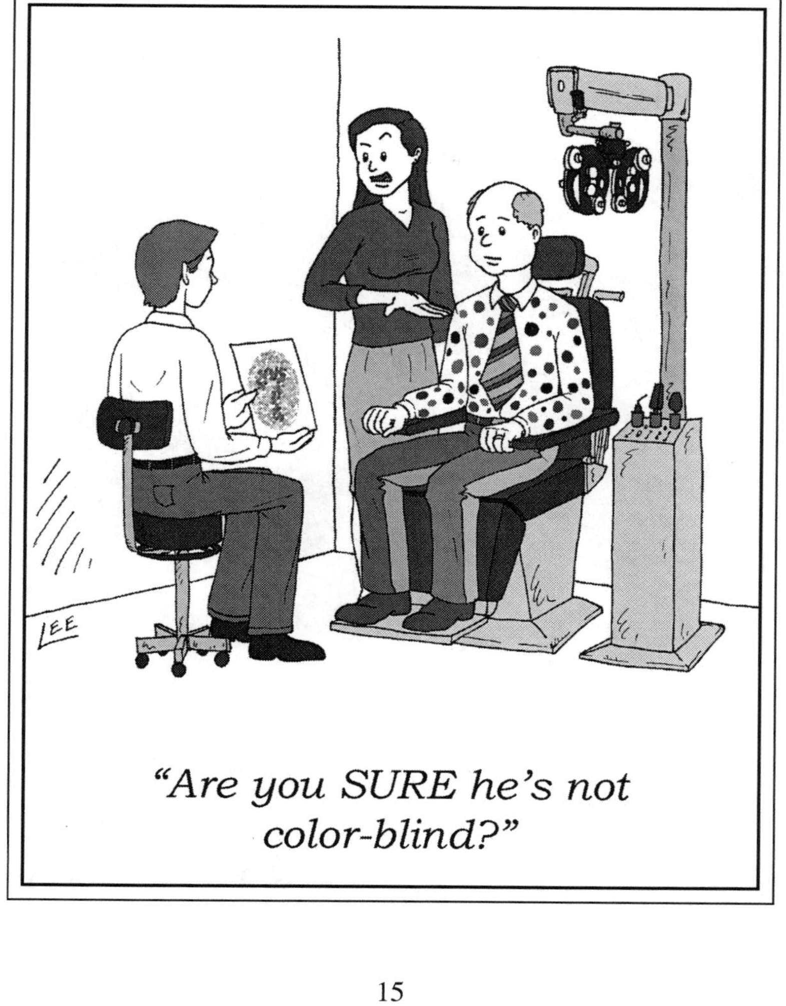
LEE

"Are you SURE he's not color-blind?"

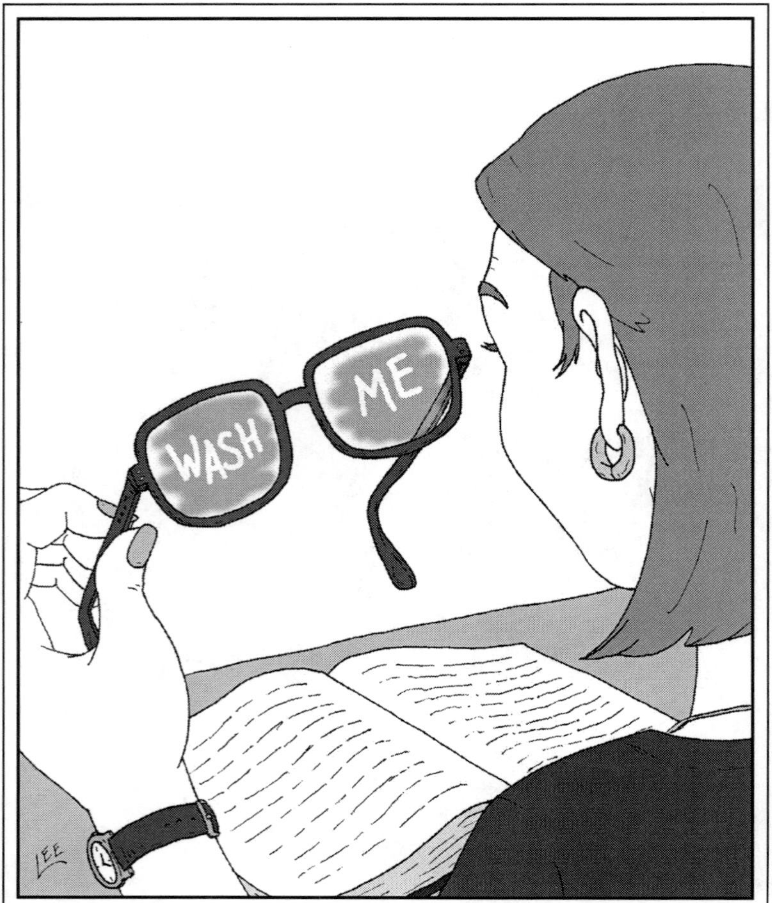
WASH
ME
LEE

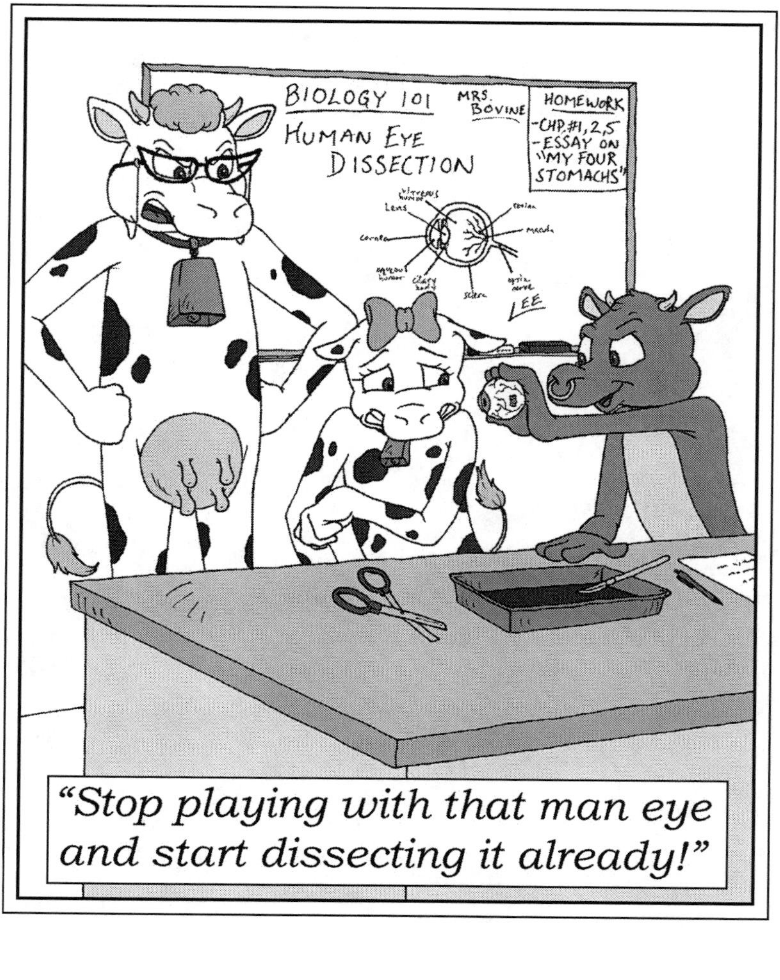
BIOLOGY 101
MRS. BOVINE
HUMAN EYE DISSECTION
HOMEWORK
-CHP.#1,2,5
-ESSAY ON "MY FOUR STOMACHS"
LEE

"Stop playing with that man eye and start dissecting it already!"

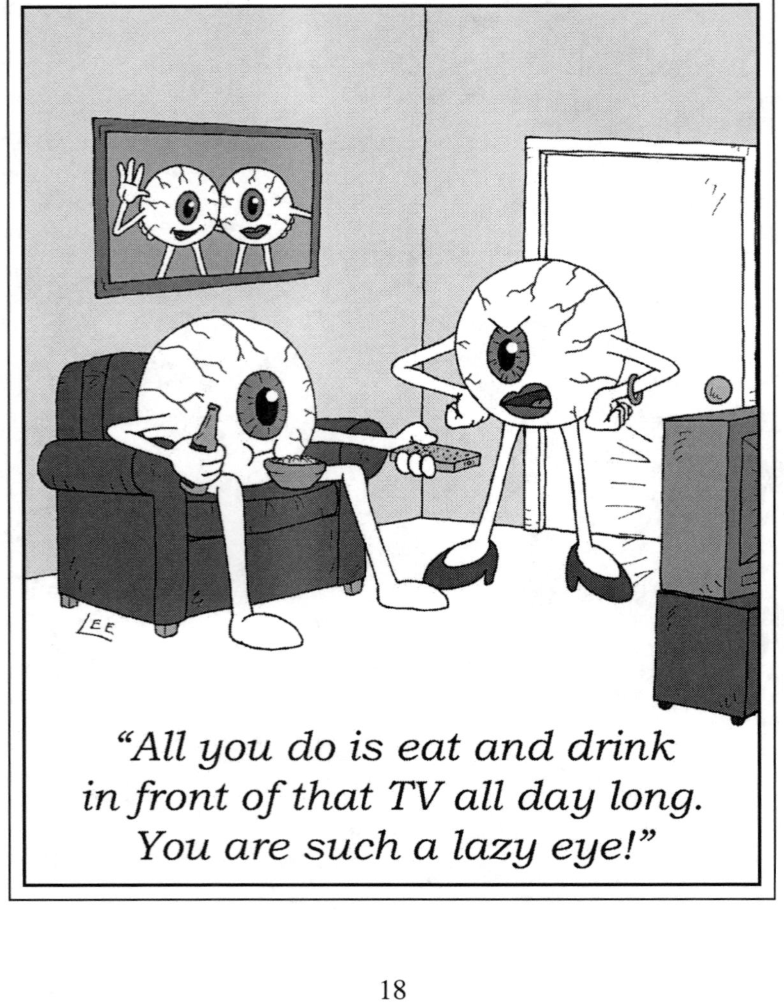
LEE

"All you do is eat and drink
in front of that TV all day long.
You are such a lazy eye!"

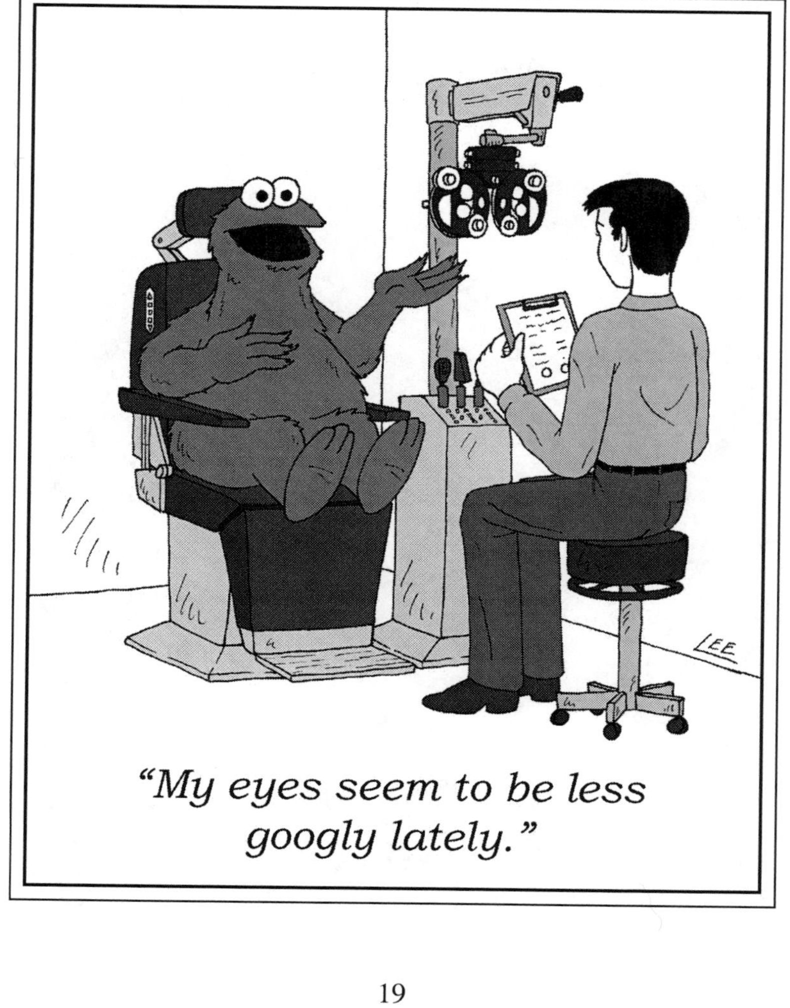
LEE

"My eyes seem to be less googly lately."

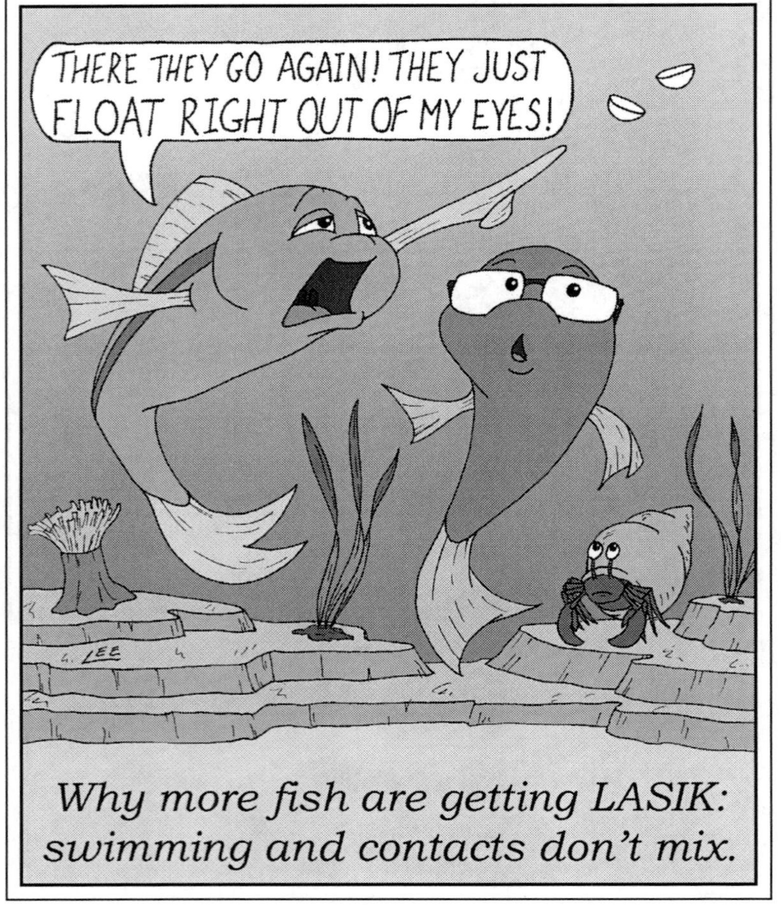
THERE THEY GO AGAIN! THEY JUST FLOAT RIGHT OUT OF MY EYES!
L. LEE

Why more fish are getting LASIK: swimming and contacts don't mix.

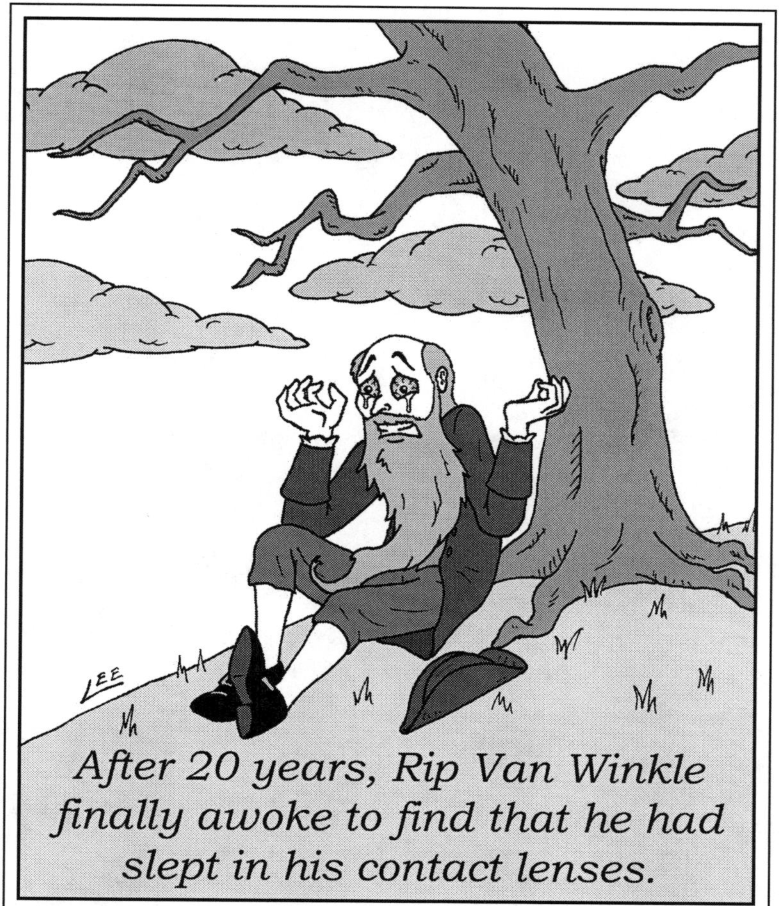
LEE
After 20 years, Rip Van Winkle finally awoke to find that he had slept in his contact lenses.

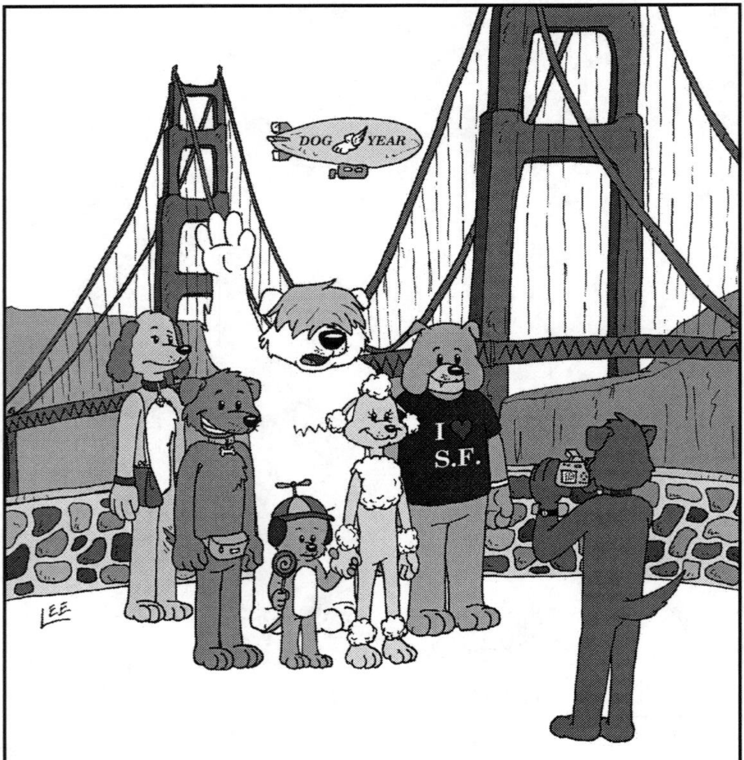
DOG YEAR
I ♥ S.F.
LEE

"Can you take that picture again? I think my eyes were closed."

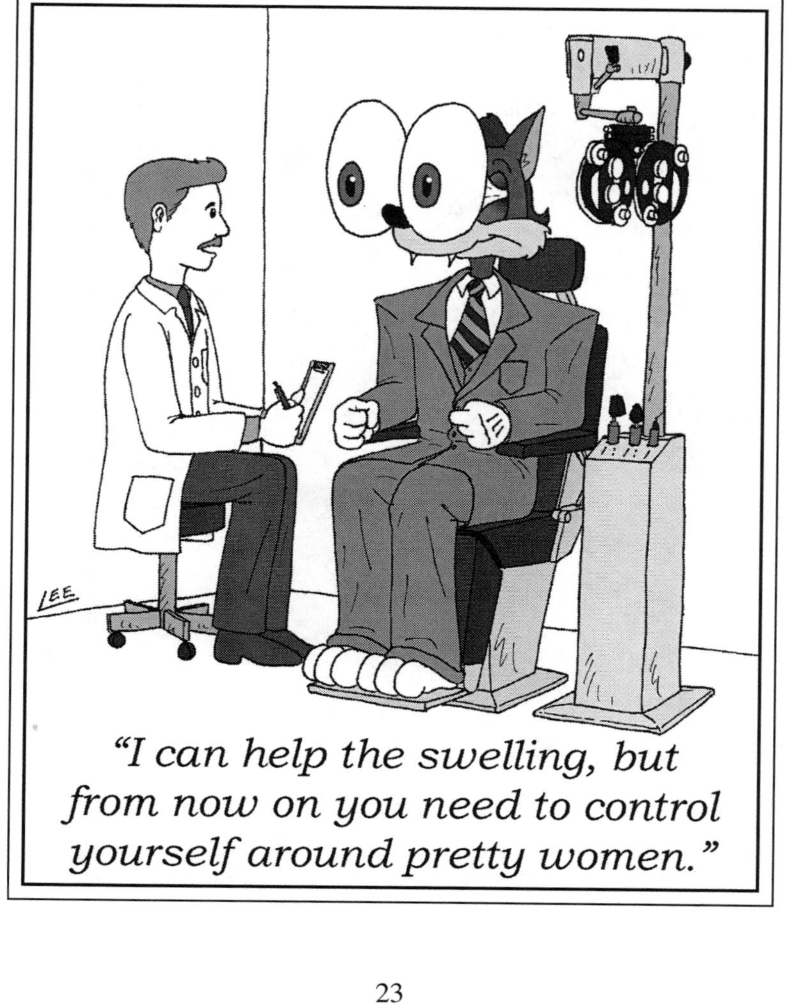
LEE

"I can help the swelling, but from now on you need to control yourself around pretty women."

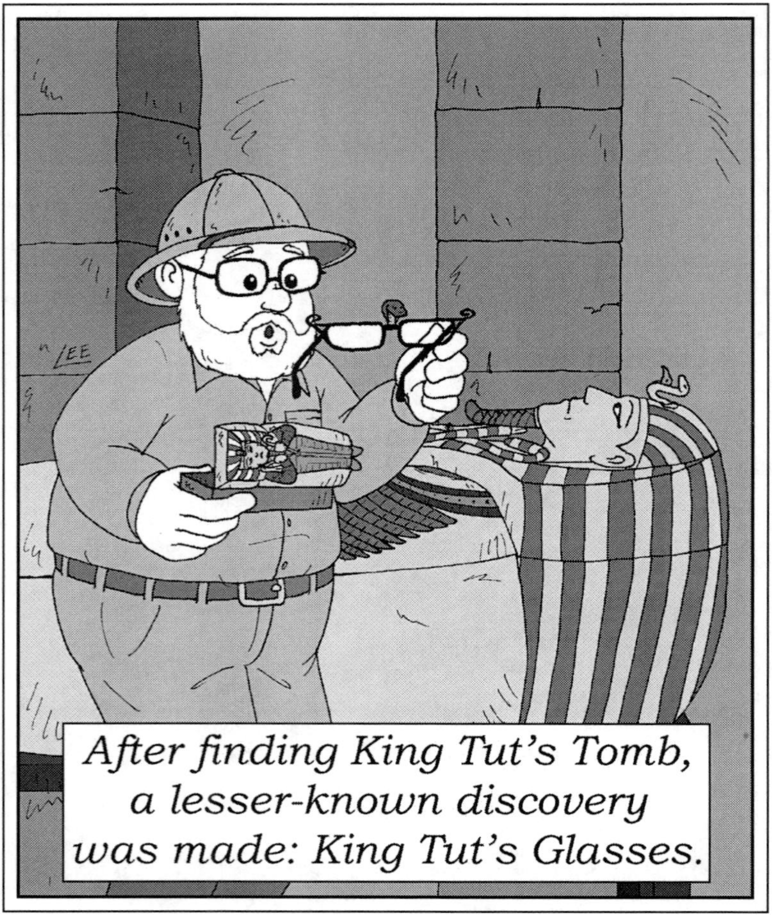
After finding King Tut's Tomb, a lesser-known discovery was made: King Tut's Glasses.

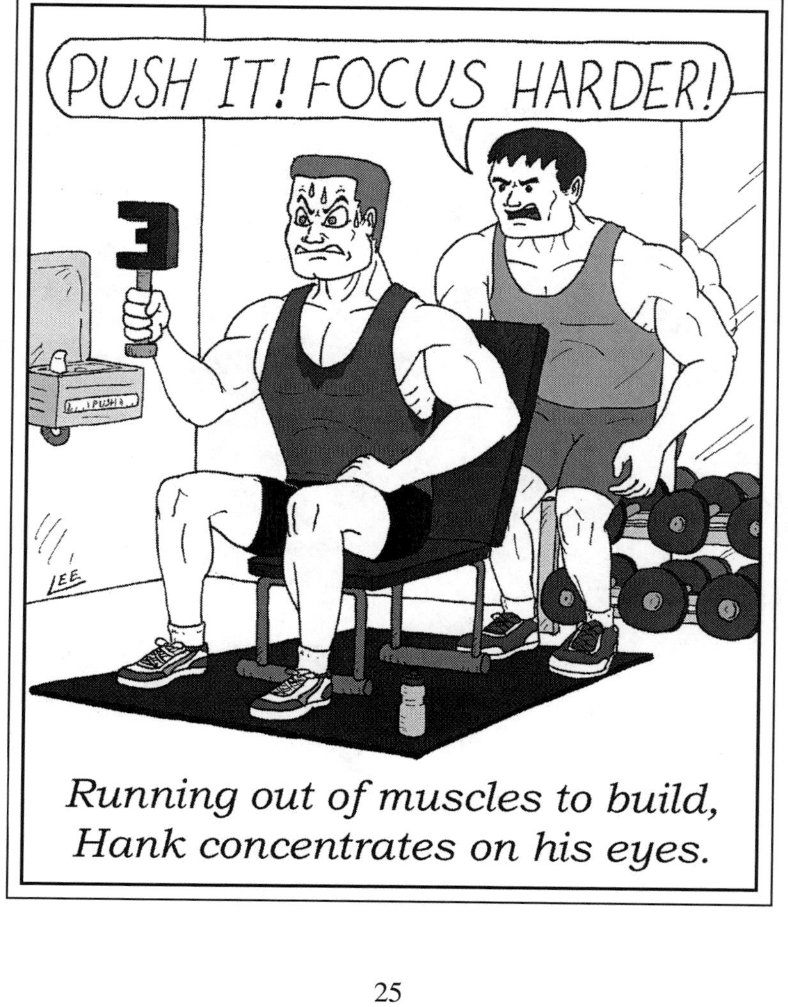
PUSH IT! FOCUS HARDER!
PUSH
LEE

Running out of muscles to build, Hank concentrates on his eyes.

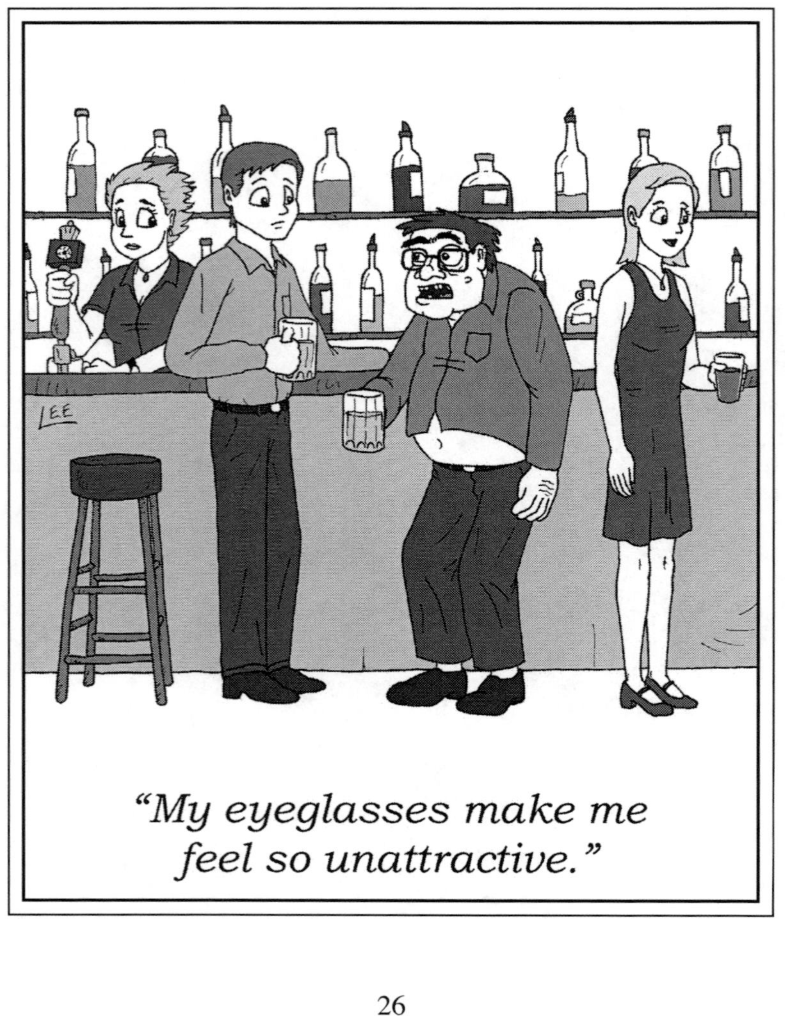
LEE

"My eyeglasses make me feel so unattractive."

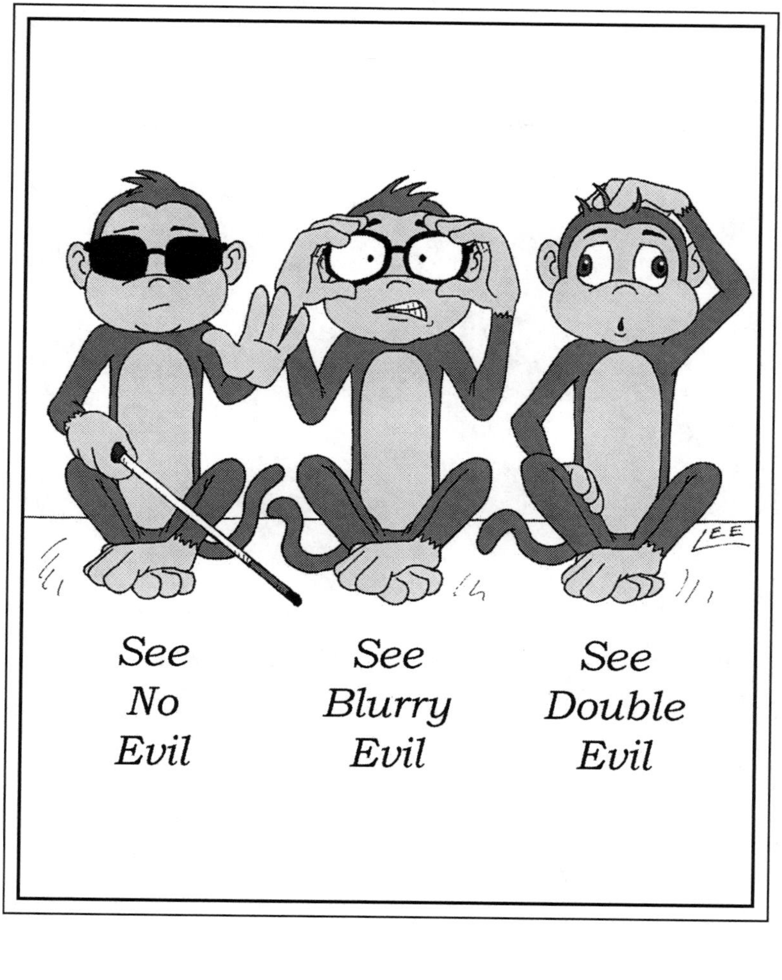
LEE
See No Evil
See Blurry Evil
See Double Evil

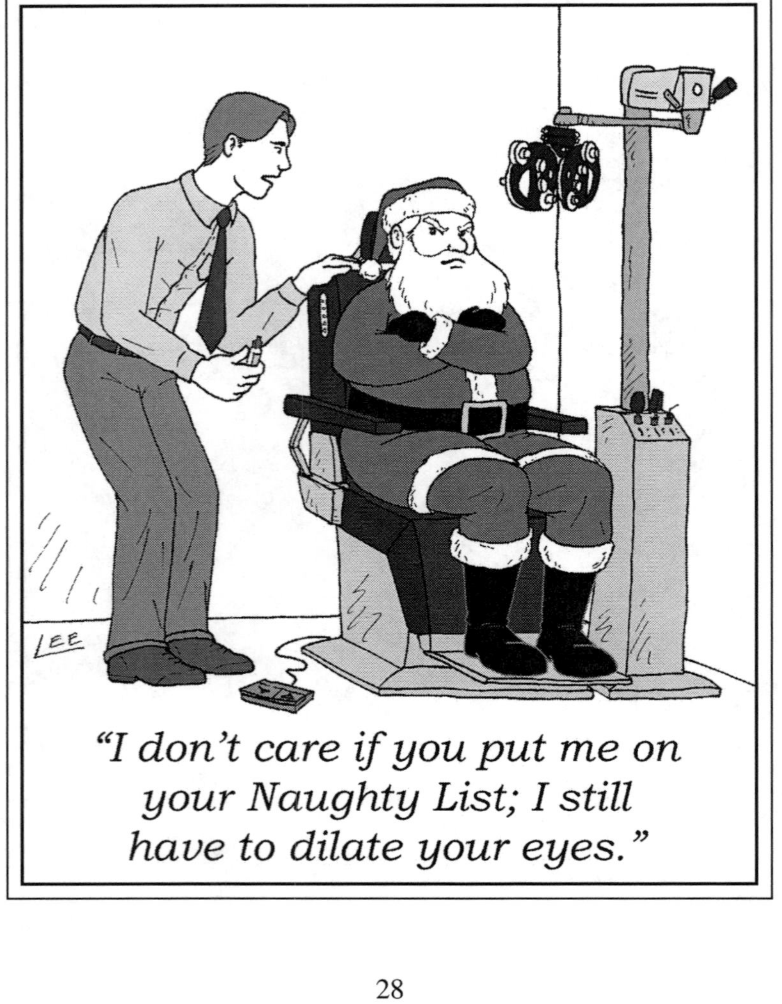
LEE

"I don't care if you put me on your Naughty List; I still have to dilate your eyes."

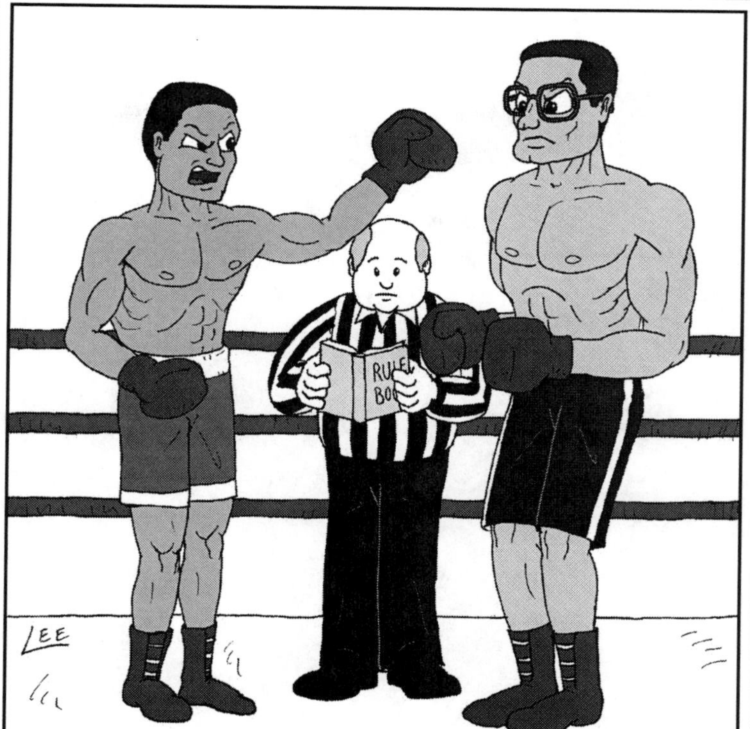
LEE

"Ohhhh, no! I'm not falling for that 'You can't hit a guy with glasses' trick again!"

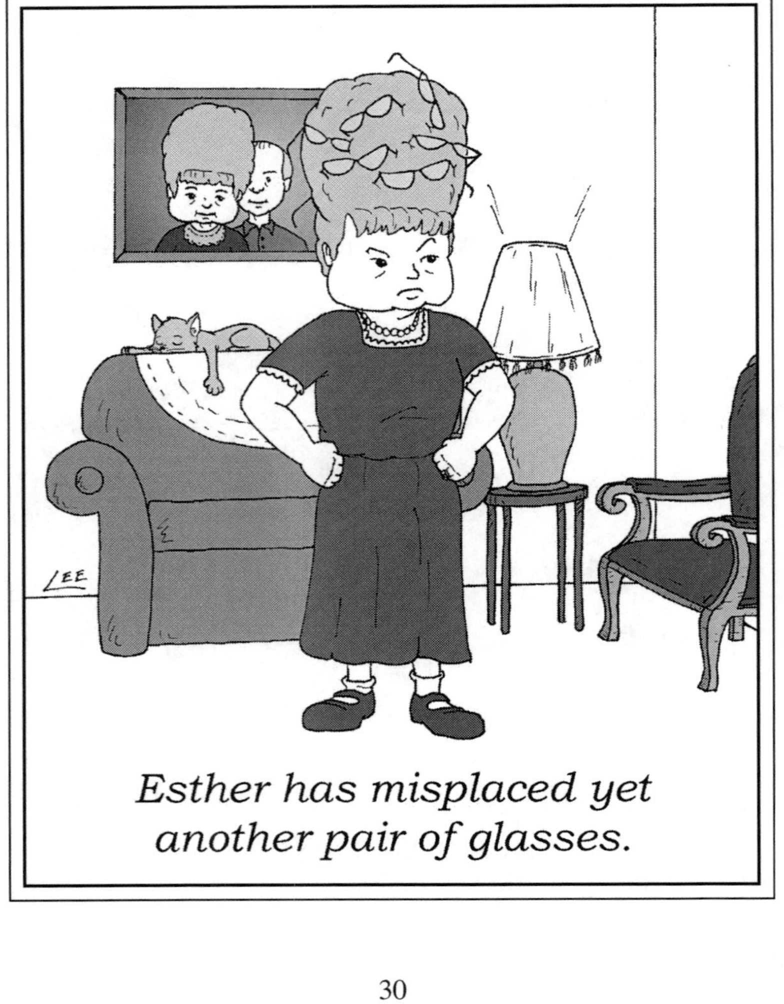
LEE

Esther has misplaced yet another pair of glasses.

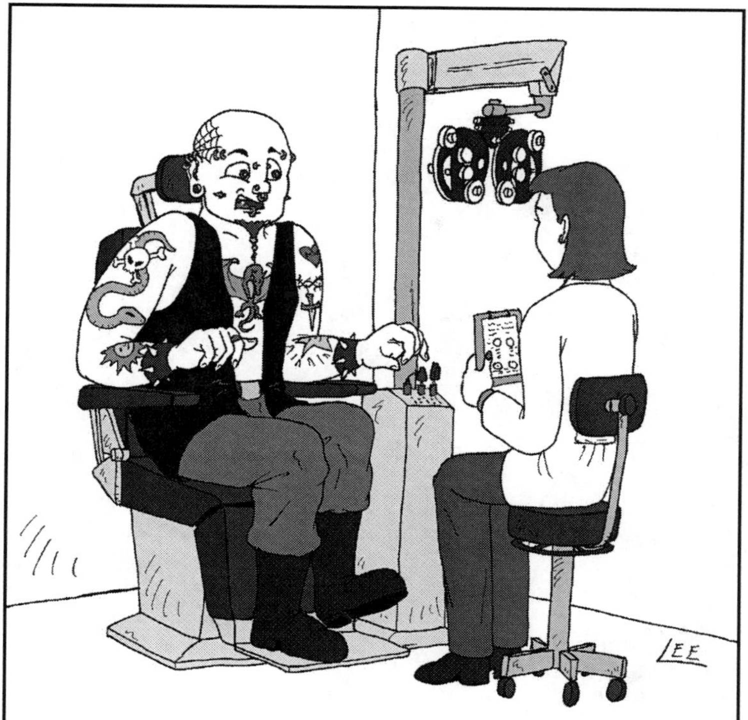
LEE

"I can't wear contacts.
The thought of sticking something
in my eye really freaks me out!"

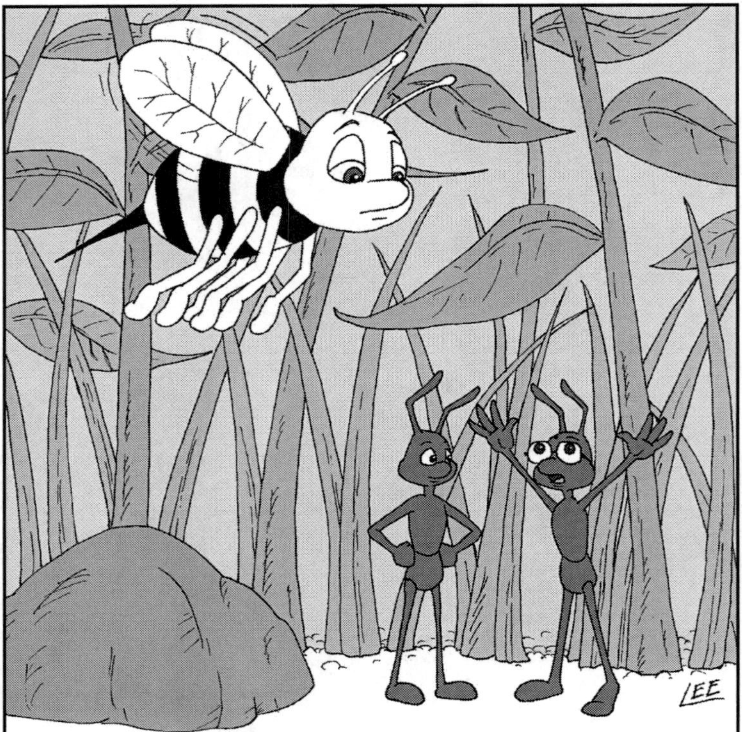
LEE

"These new glasses are strange. They make everything look so big!"

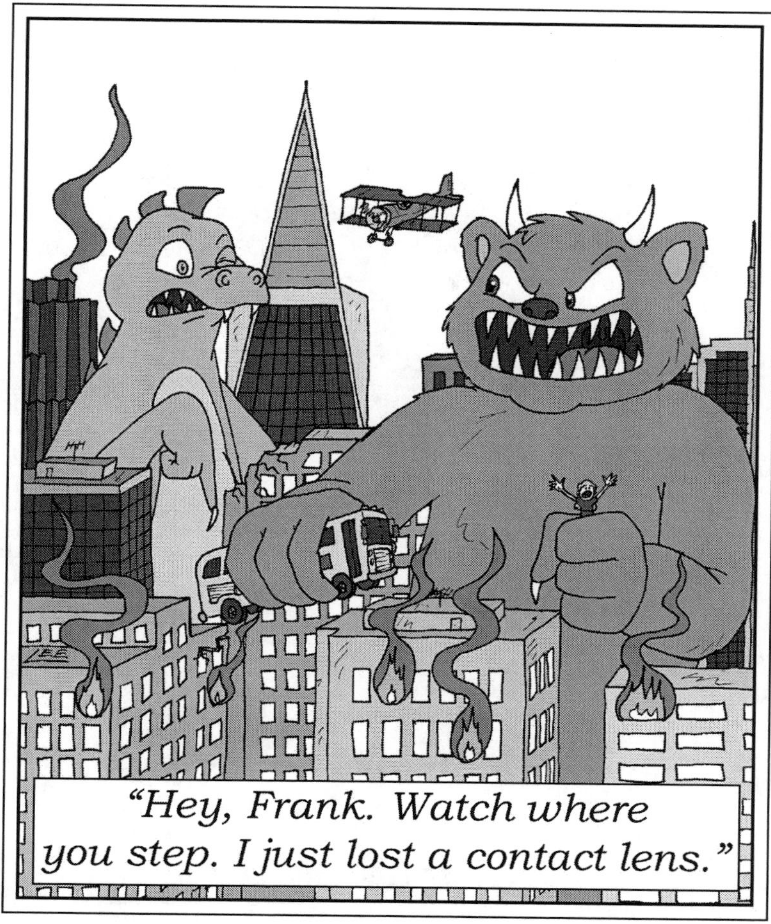

"Hey, Frank. Watch where you step. I just lost a contact lens."

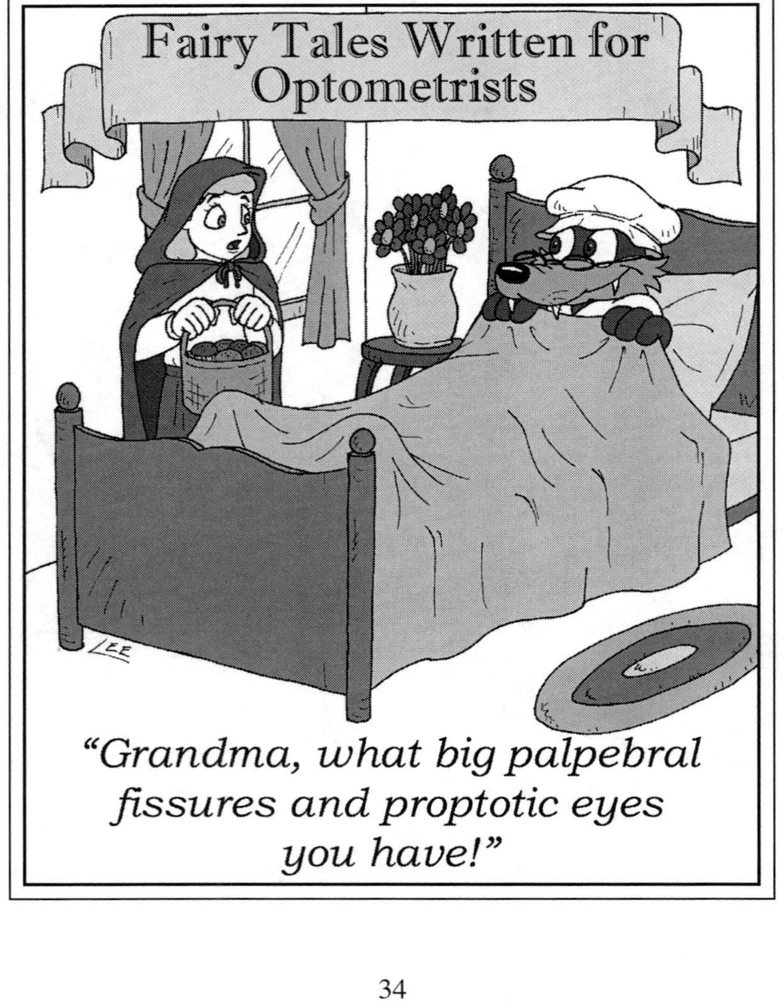
Fairy Tales Written for Optometrists
LEE

"Grandma, what big palpebral fissures and proptotic eyes you have!"

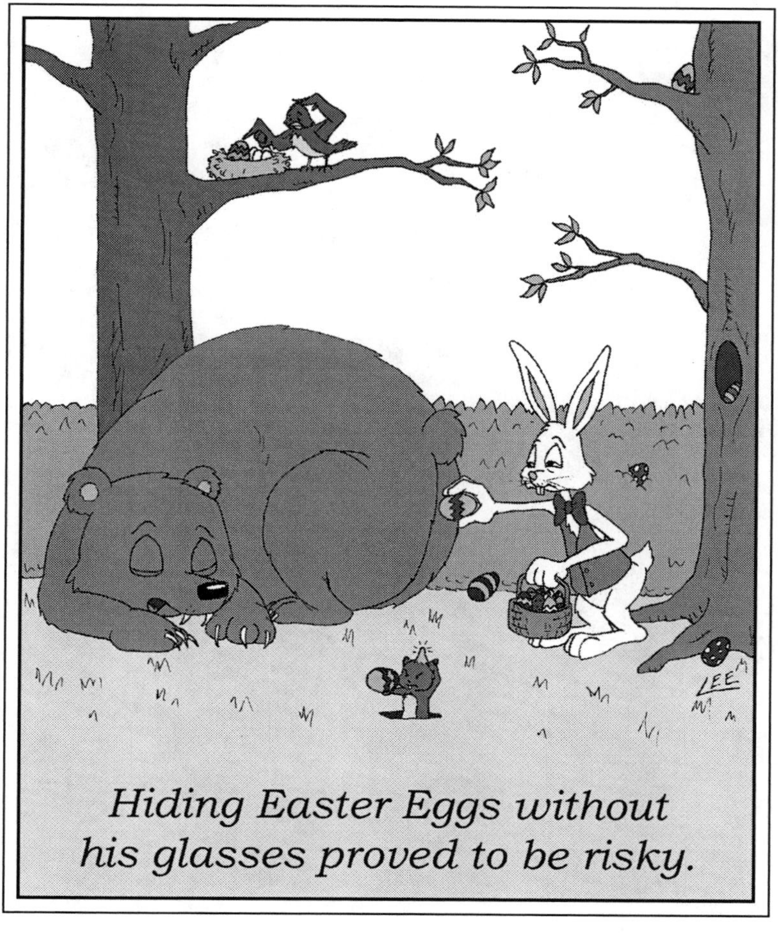
LEE

Hiding Easter Eggs without his glasses proved to be risky.

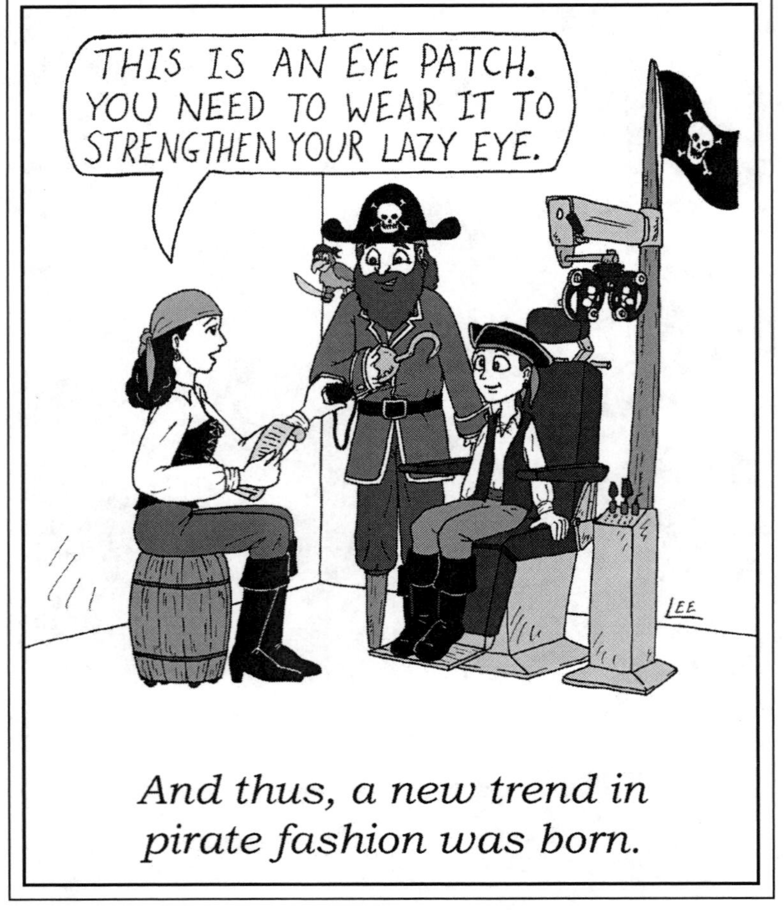
THIS IS AN EYE PATCH. YOU NEED TO WEAR IT TO STRENGTHEN YOUR LAZY EYE.
LEE

And thus, a new trend in pirate fashion was born.

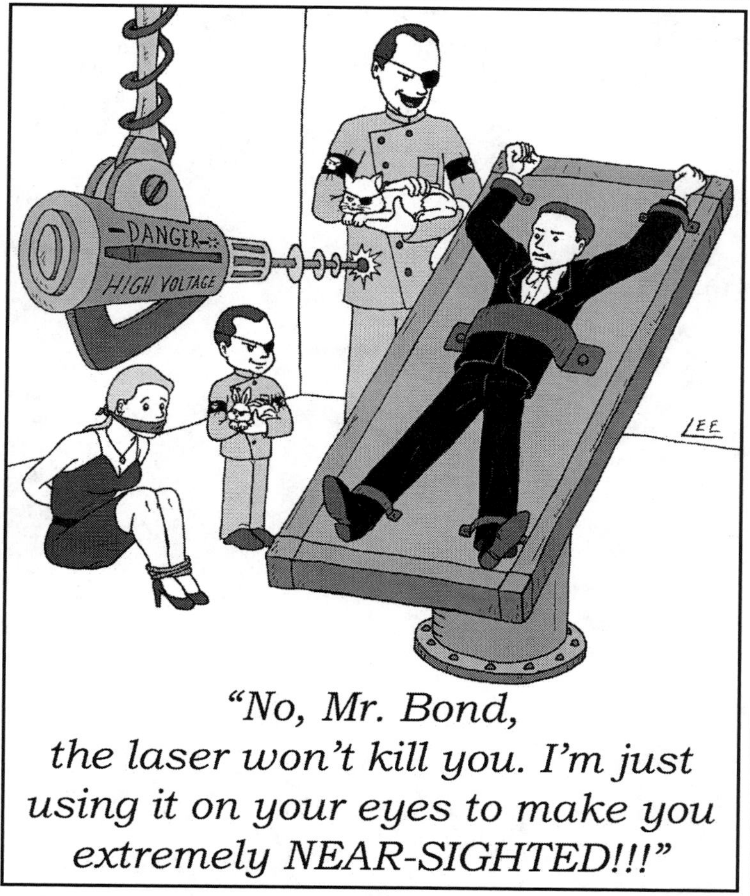
DANGER
HIGH VOLTAGE
LEE

*"No, Mr. Bond,
the laser won't kill you. I'm just
using it on your eyes to make you
extremely NEAR-SIGHTED!!!"*

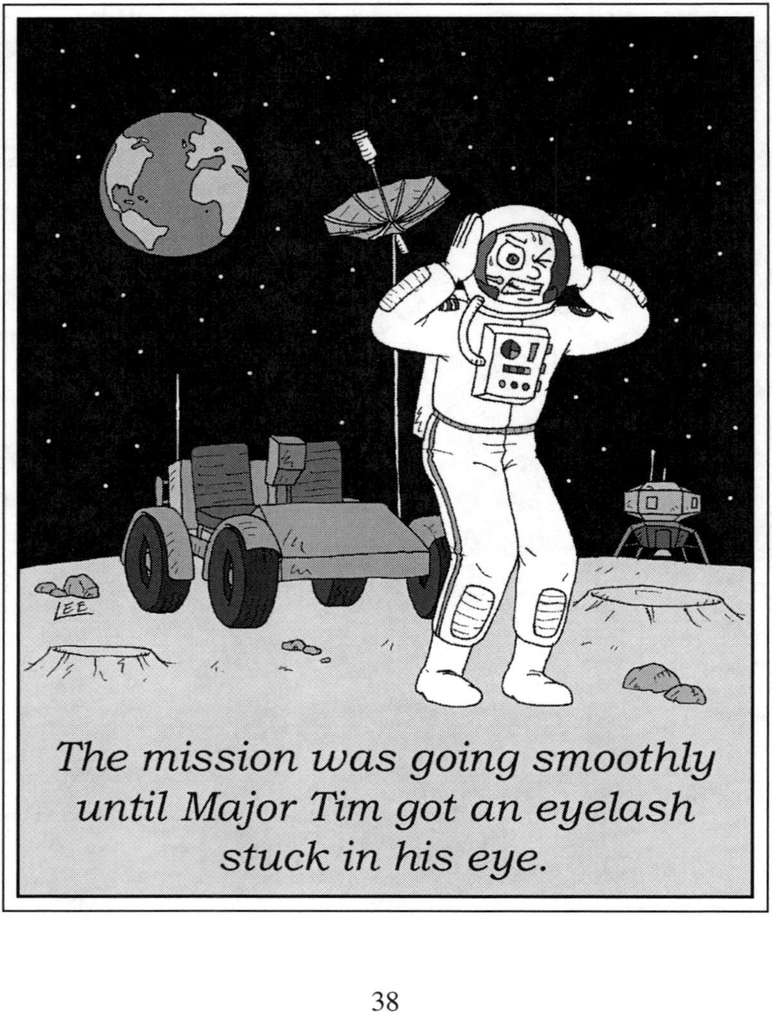
LEE

The mission was going smoothly until Major Tim got an eyelash stuck in his eye.

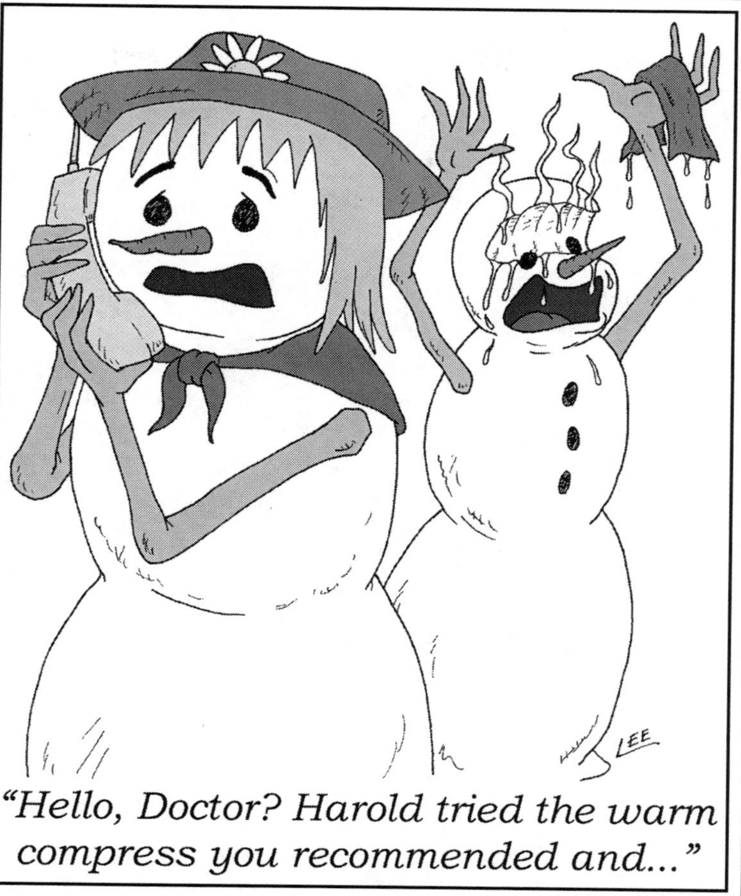
LEE

"Hello, Doctor? Harold tried the warm compress you recommended and..."

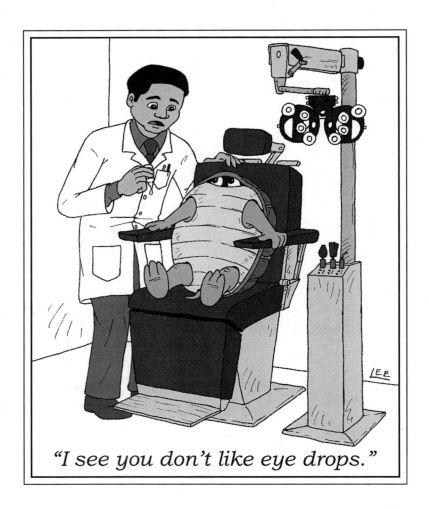

"I see you don't like eye drops."

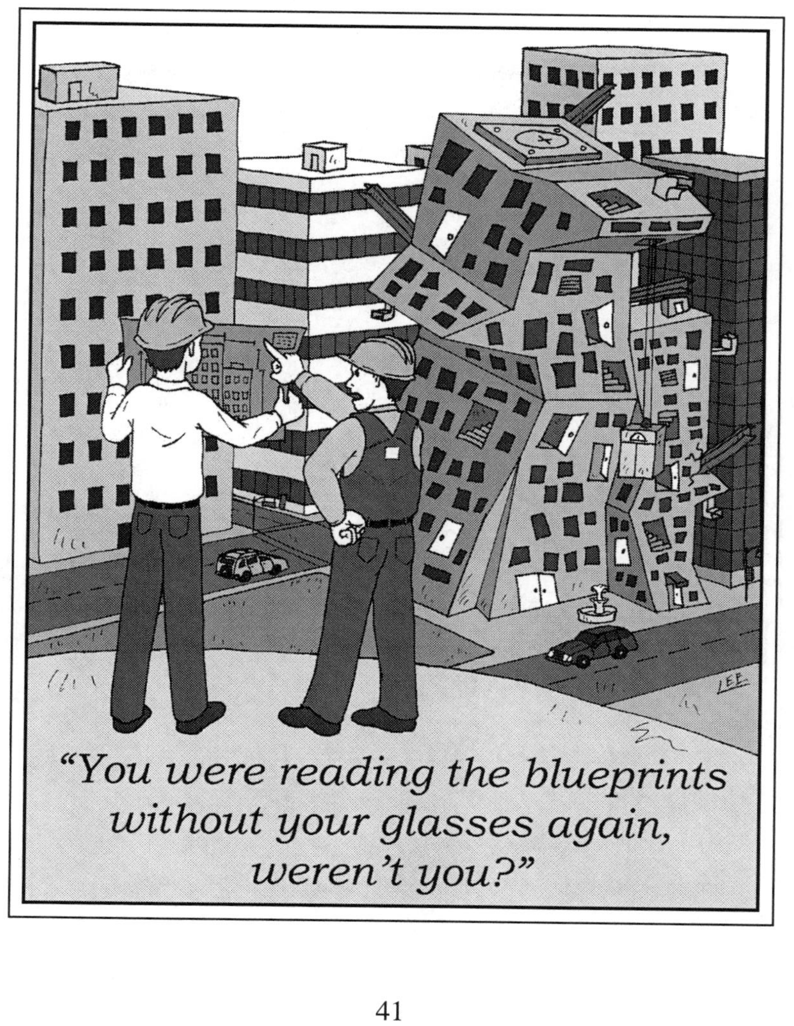
LEE

"You were reading the blueprints without your glasses again, weren't you?"

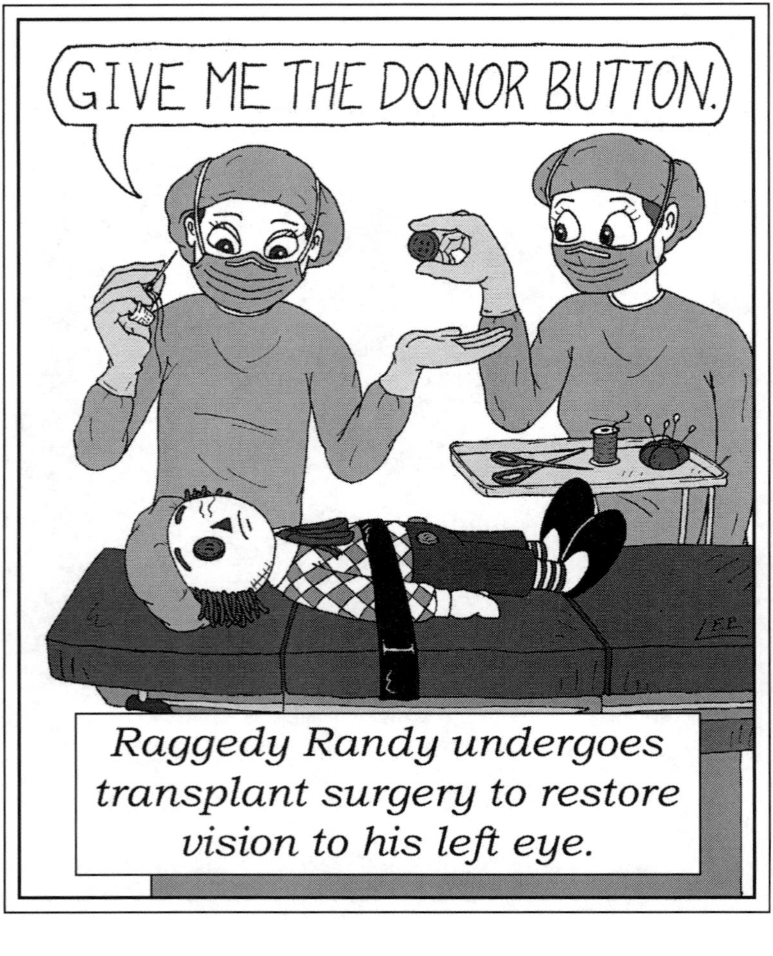

GIVE ME THE DONOR BUTTON.

Raggedy Randy undergoes transplant surgery to restore vision to his left eye.

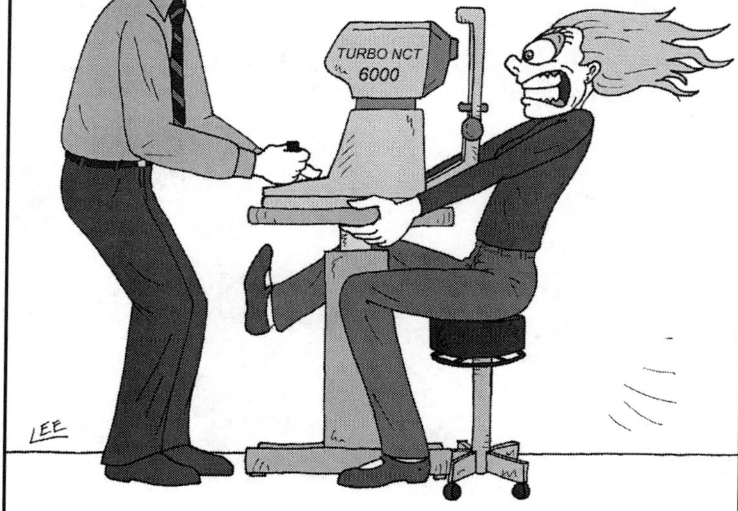
TURBO NCT
6000
LEE

Unbeknownst to Dr. Thornton, the air puff test was set to "Hurricane Blast".

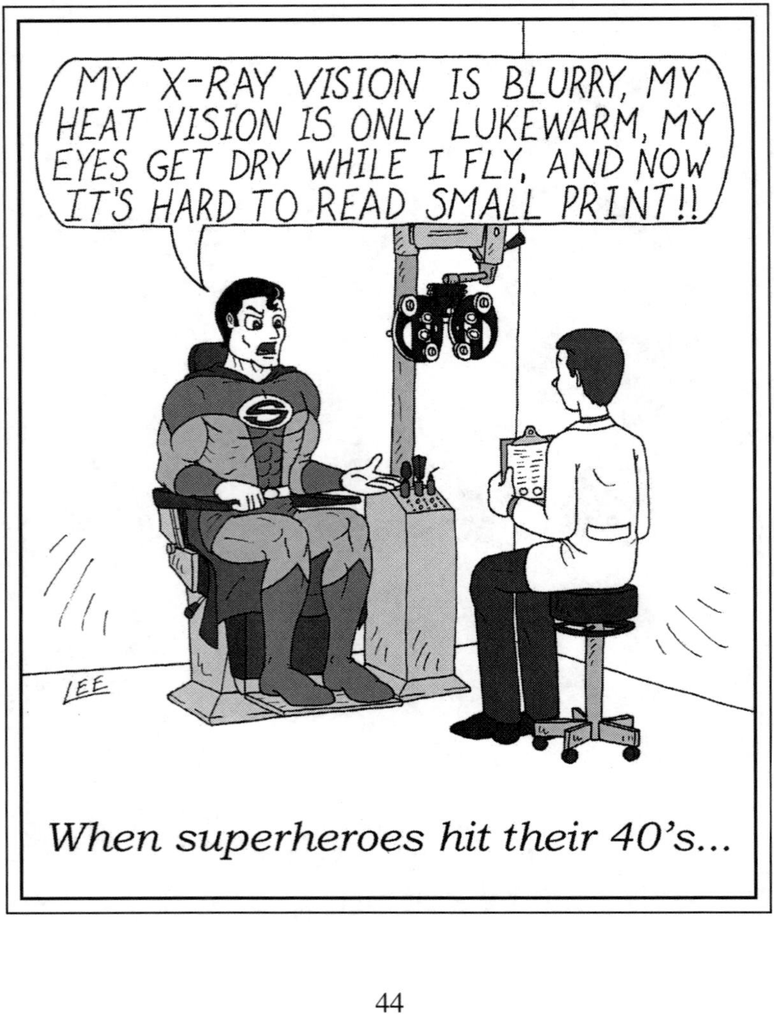
MY X-RAY VISION IS BLURRY, MY HEAT VISION IS ONLY LUKEWARM, MY EYES GET DRY WHILE I FLY, AND NOW IT'S HARD TO READ SMALL PRINT!!
LEE

When superheroes hit their 40's...

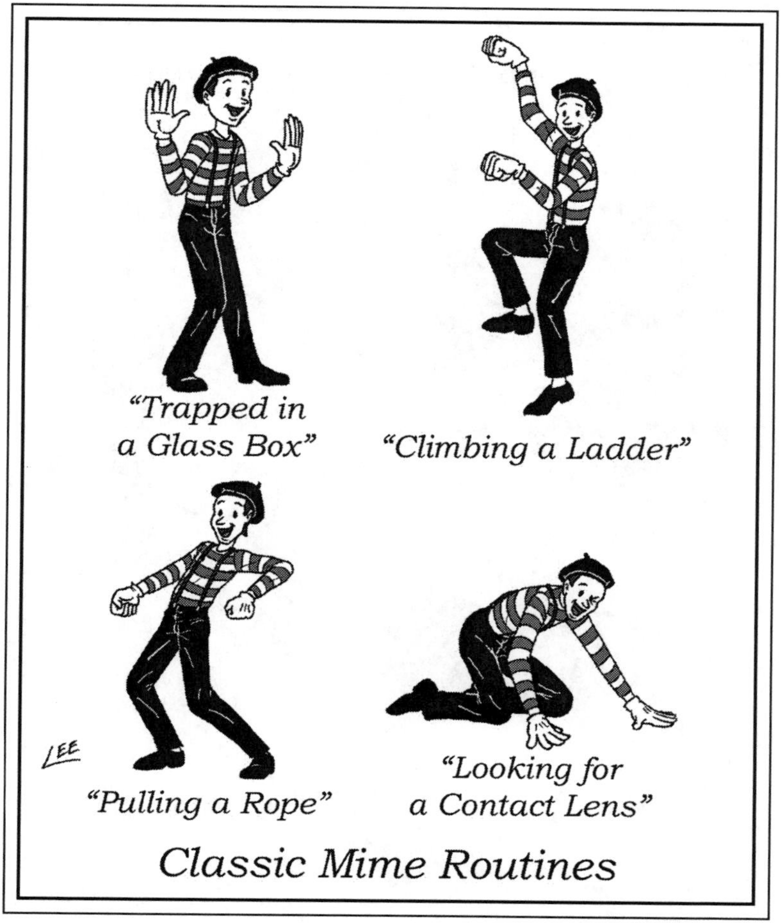
"Trapped in
a Glass Box"
"Climbing a Ladder"
LEE
"Pulling a Rope"
"Looking for
a Contact Lens"

Classic Mime Routines

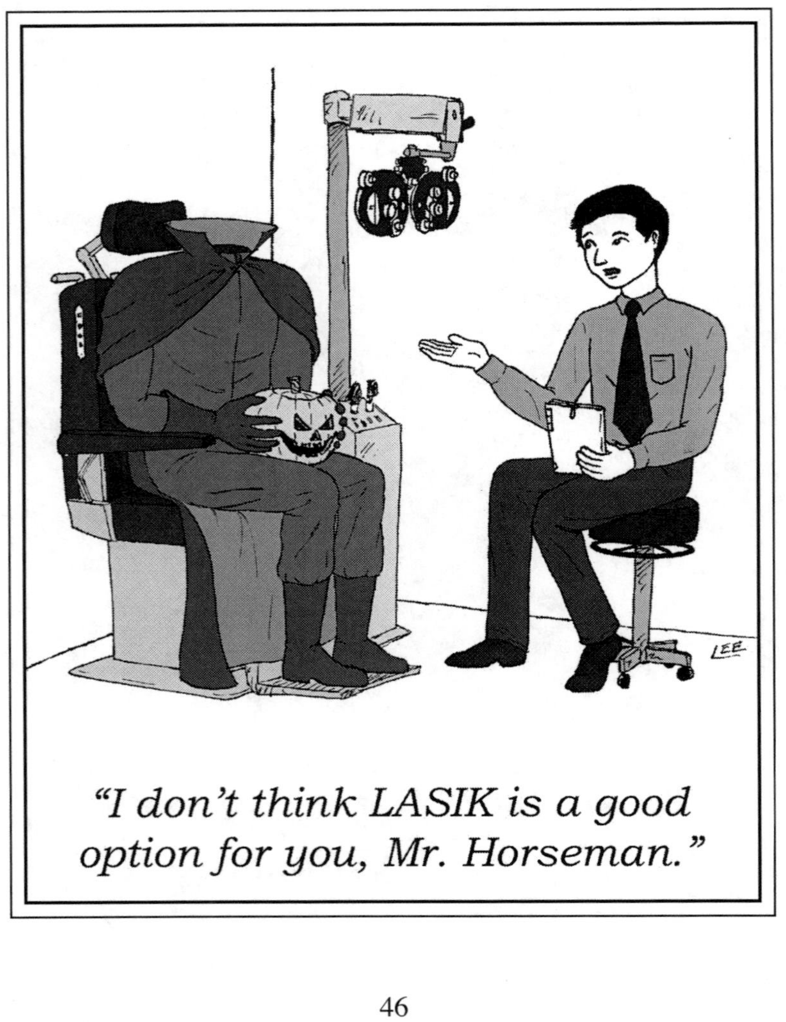
LEE

"I don't think LASIK is a good option for you, Mr. Horseman."

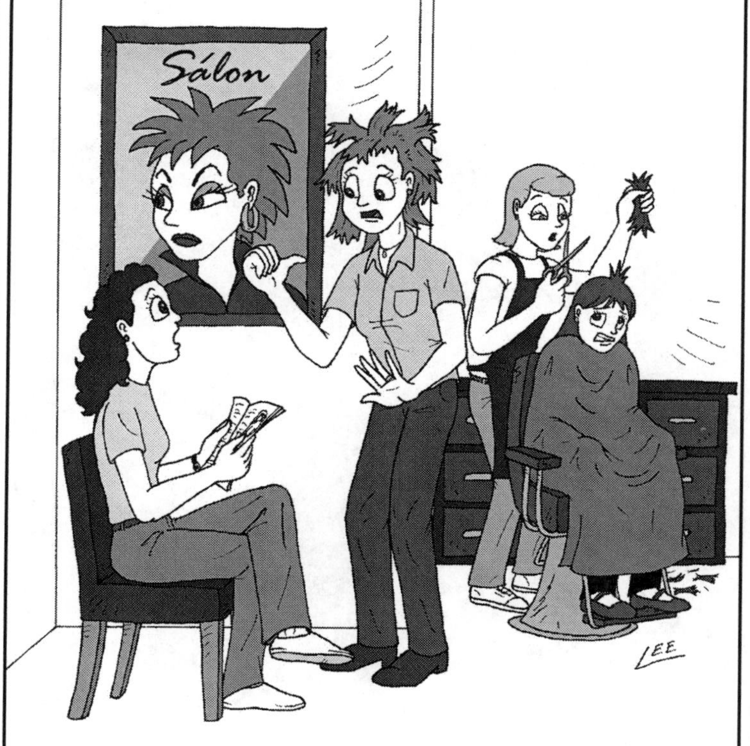
Sálon
LEE

*"Make a run for it!
The stylist lost her glasses."*

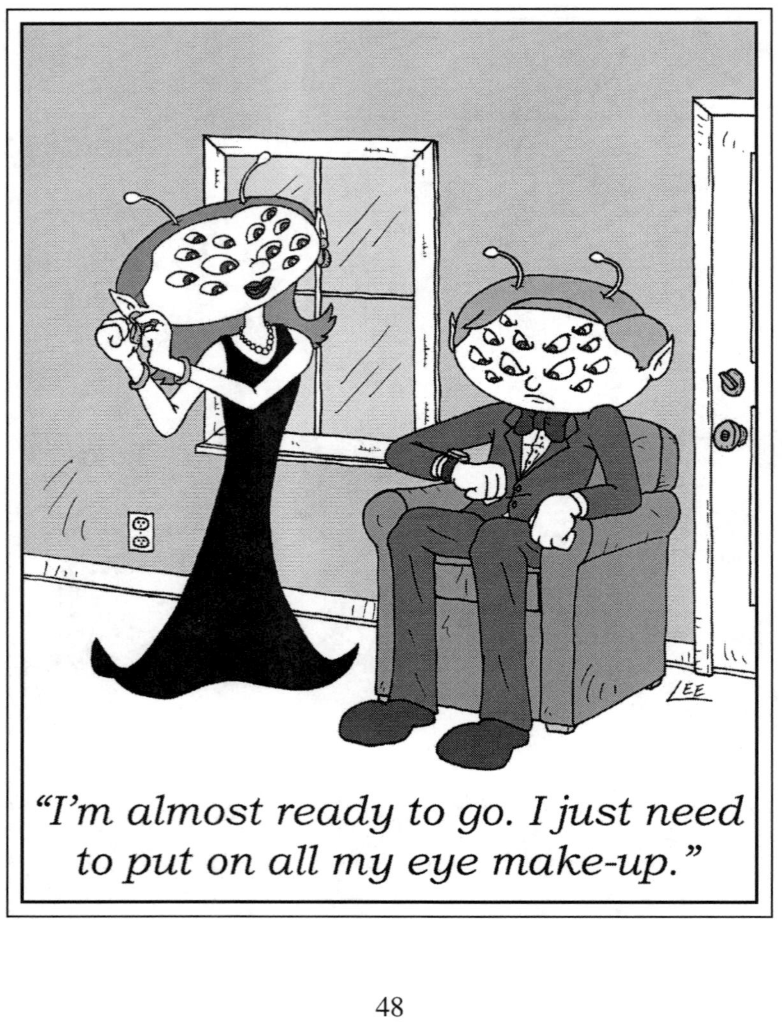
LEE

"I'm almost ready to go. I just need to put on all my eye make-up."

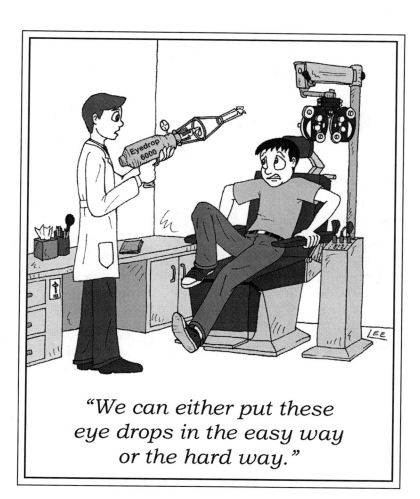

"We can either put these eye drops in the easy way or the hard way."

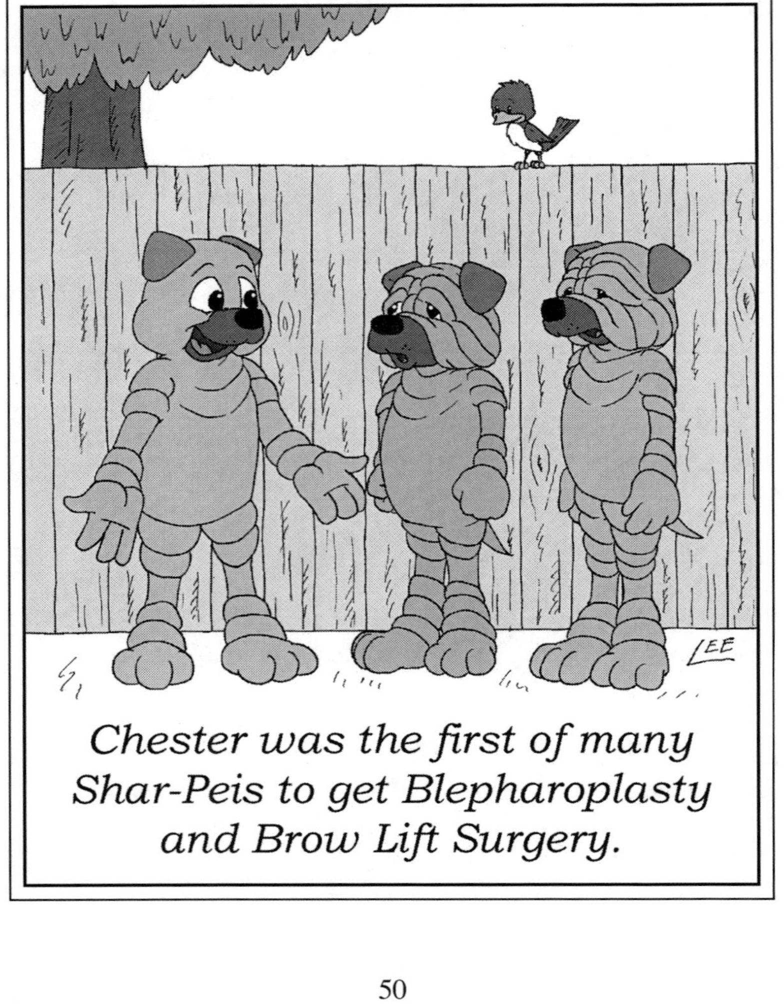
LEE

Chester was the first of many Shar-Peis to get Blepharoplasty and Brow Lift Surgery.

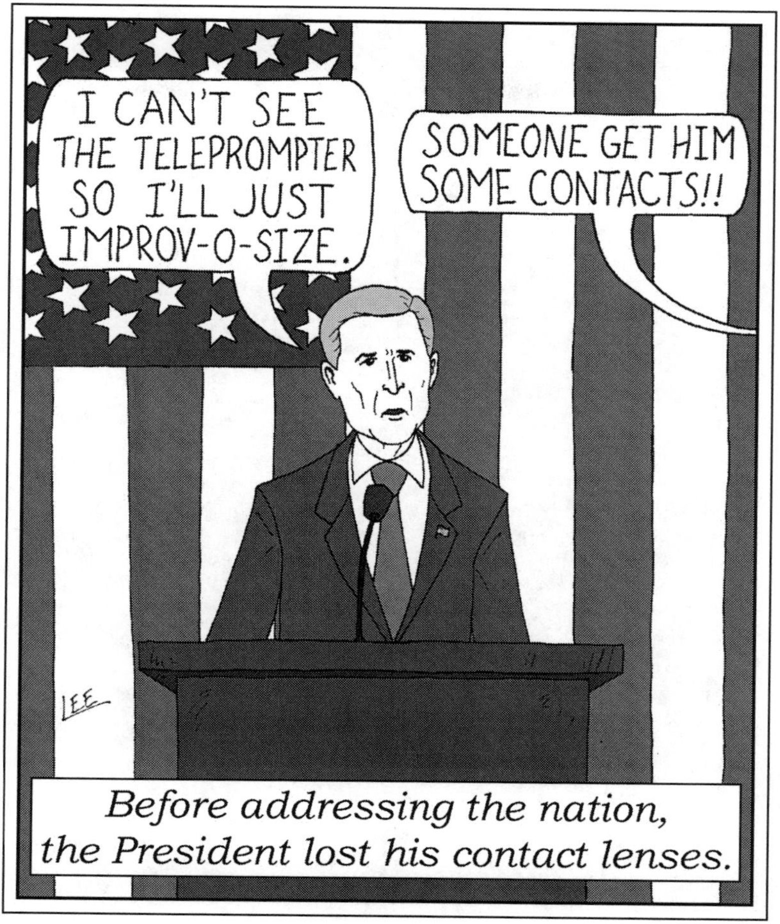
I CAN'T SEE THE TELEPROMPTER SO I'LL JUST IMPROV-O-SIZE.
SOMEONE GET HIM SOME CONTACTS!!
LEE

Before addressing the nation, the President lost his contact lenses.

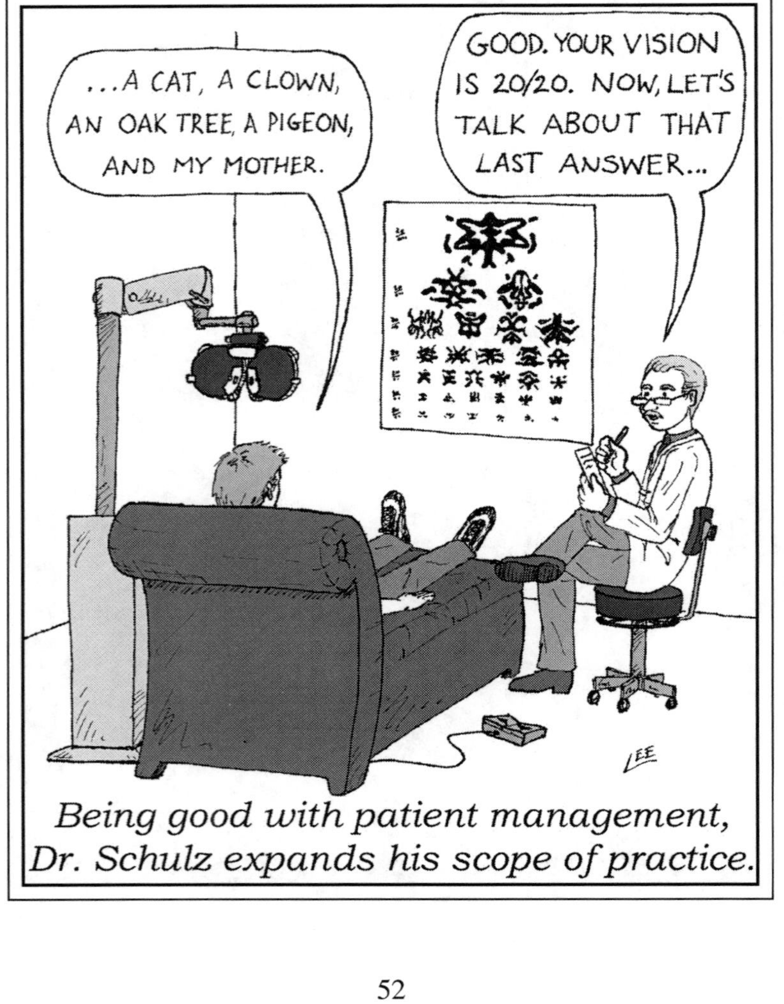
...A CAT, A CLOWN, AN OAK TREE, A PIGEON, AND MY MOTHER.
GOOD. YOUR VISION IS 20/20. NOW, LET'S TALK ABOUT THAT LAST ANSWER...
LEE

Being good with patient management, Dr. Schulz expands his scope of practice.

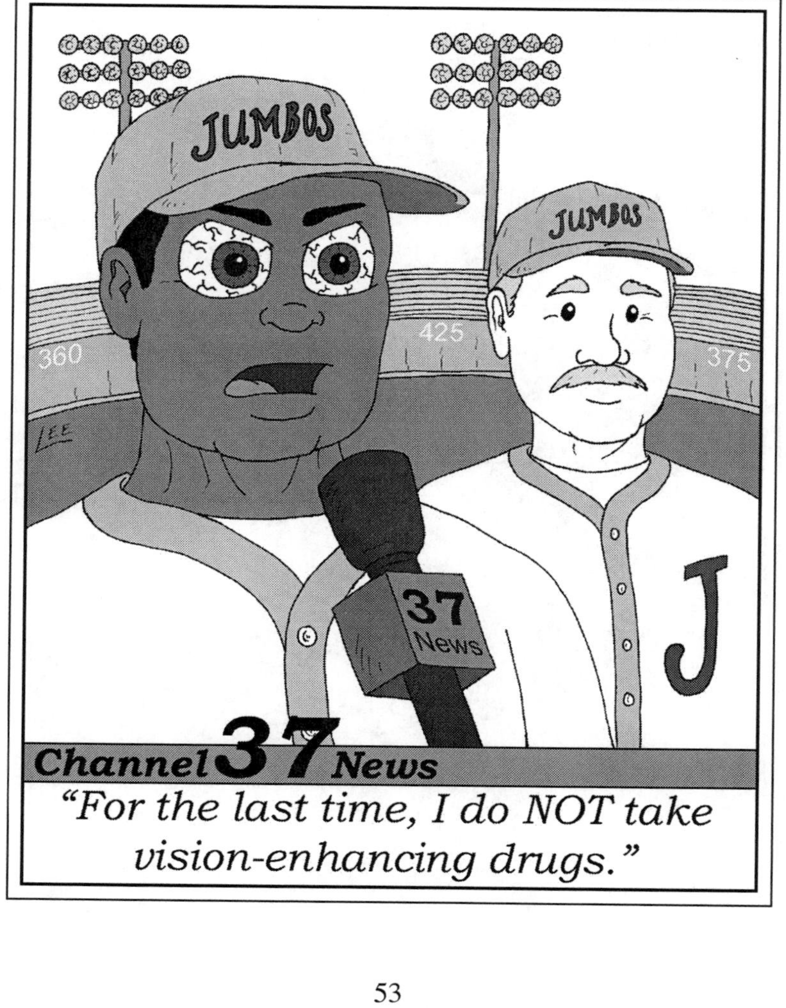
JUMBOS
JUMBOS
360
425
375
LEE
37
News
J
Channel 37 News

"For the last time, I do NOT take vision-enhancing drugs."

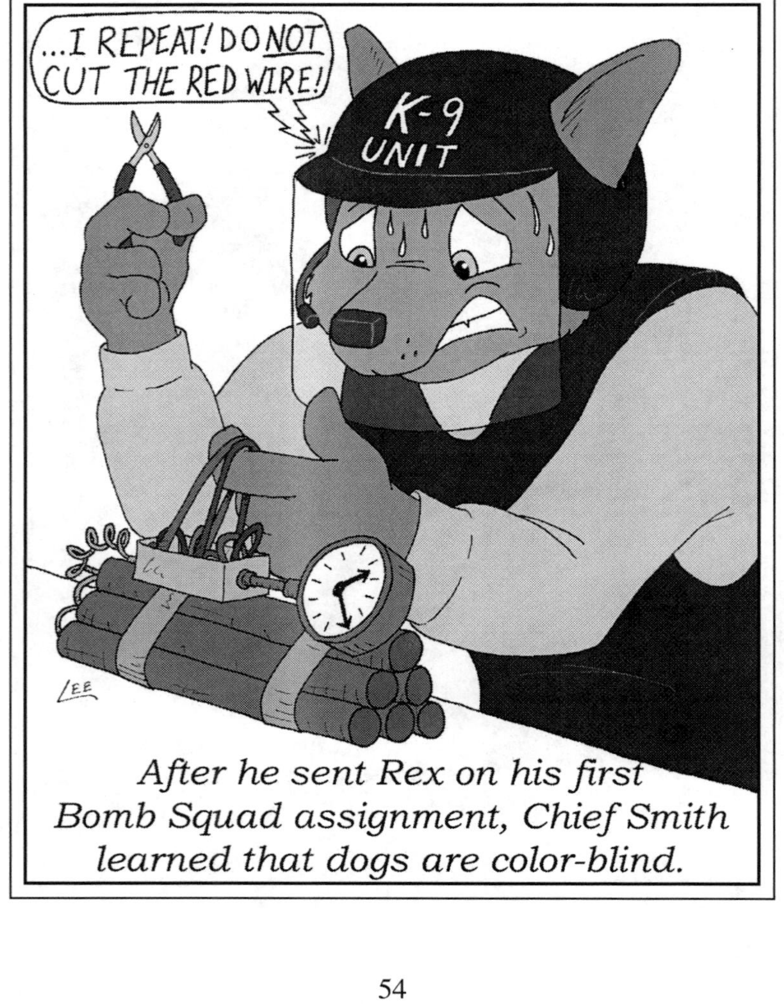
...I REPEAT! DO NOT CUT THE RED WIRE!
K-9 UNIT
LEE

After he sent Rex on his first Bomb Squad assignment, Chief Smith learned that dogs are color-blind.

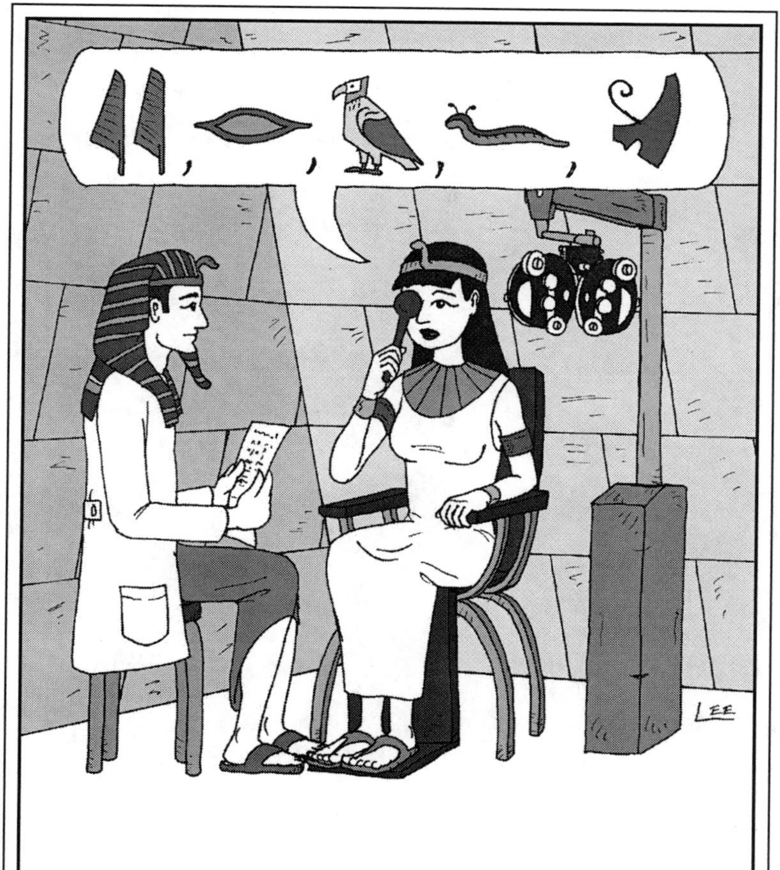
LEE

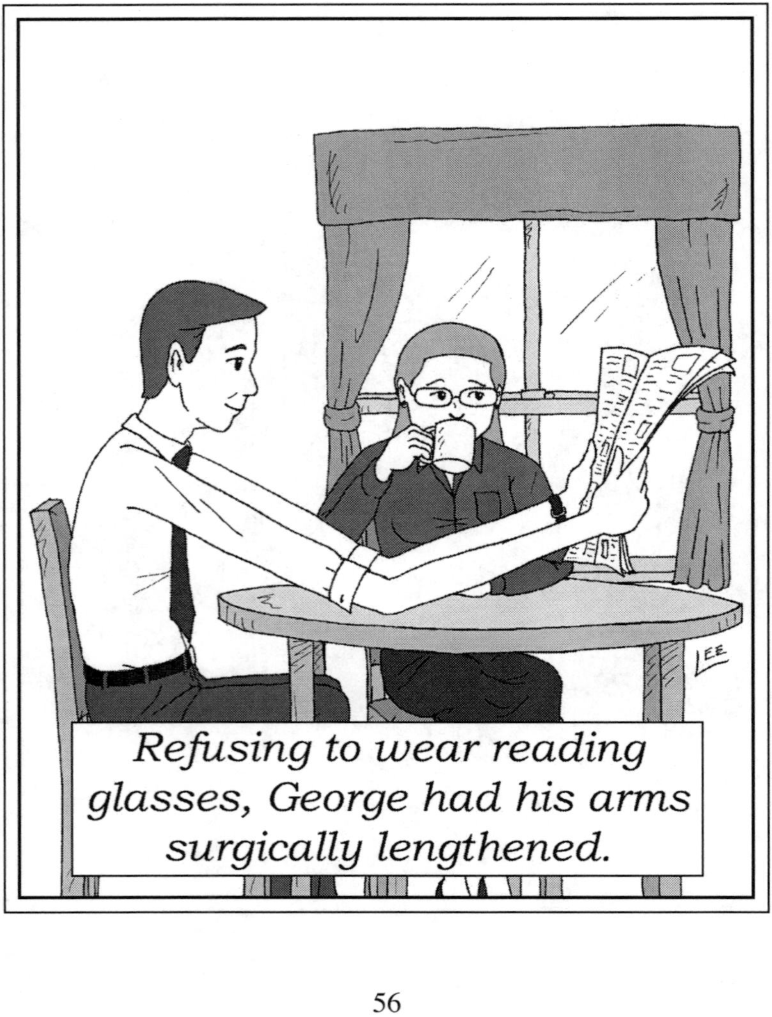
LEE

Refusing to wear reading glasses, George had his arms surgically lengthened.

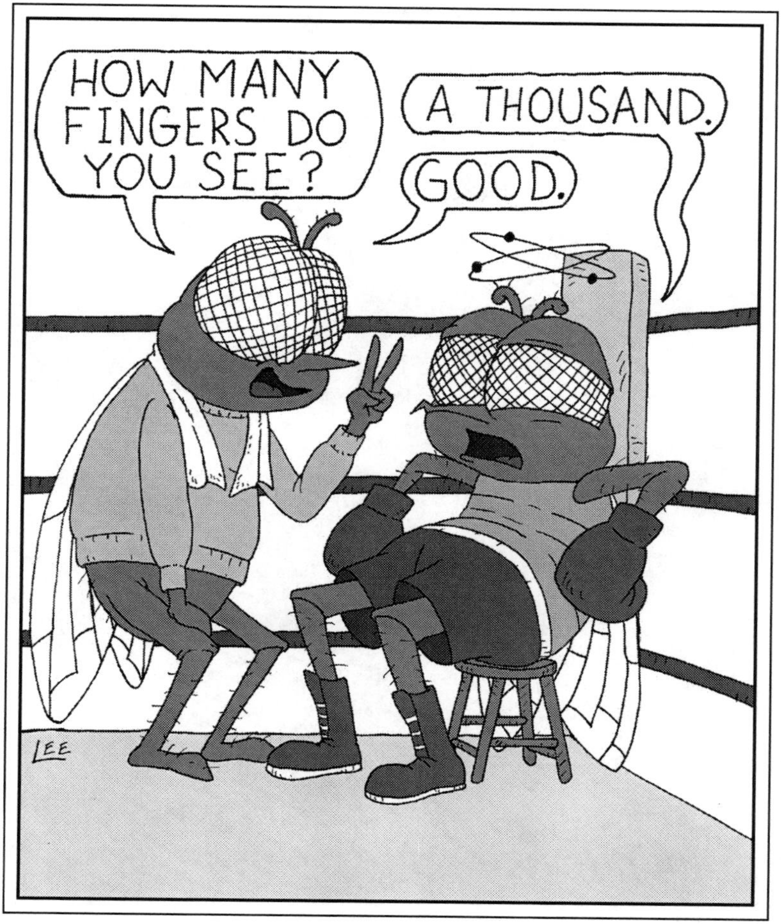
HOW MANY FINGERS DO YOU SEE?
A THOUSAND.
GOOD.
LEE

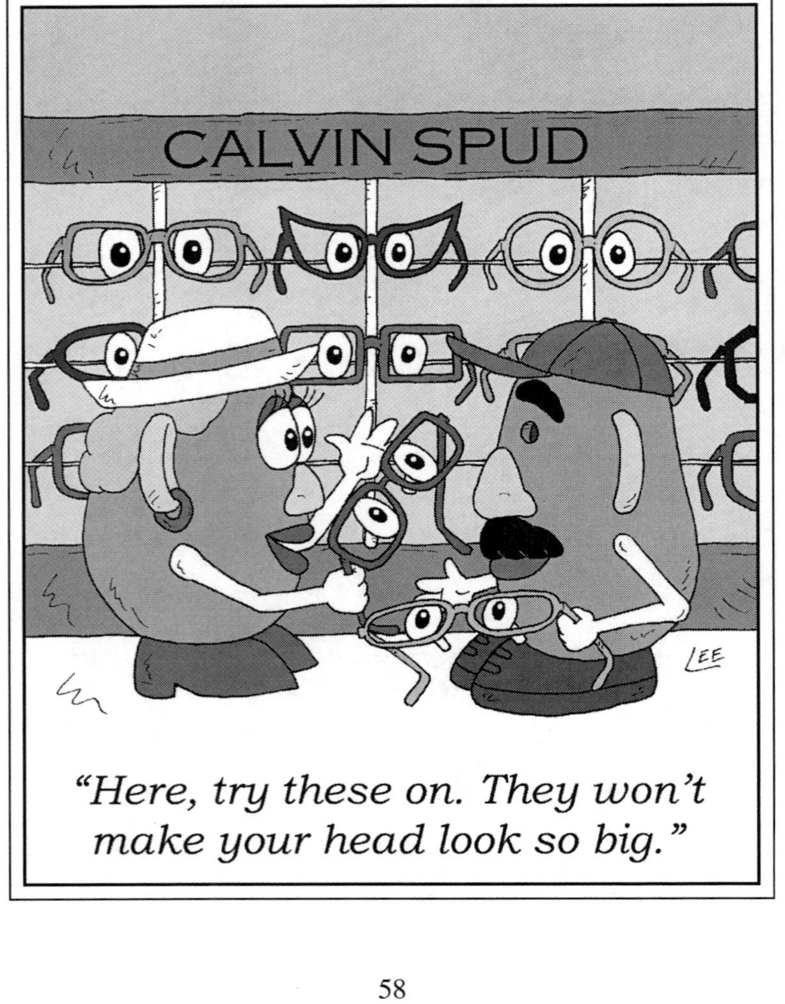
CALVIN SPUD
LEE

"Here, try these on. They won't make your head look so big."

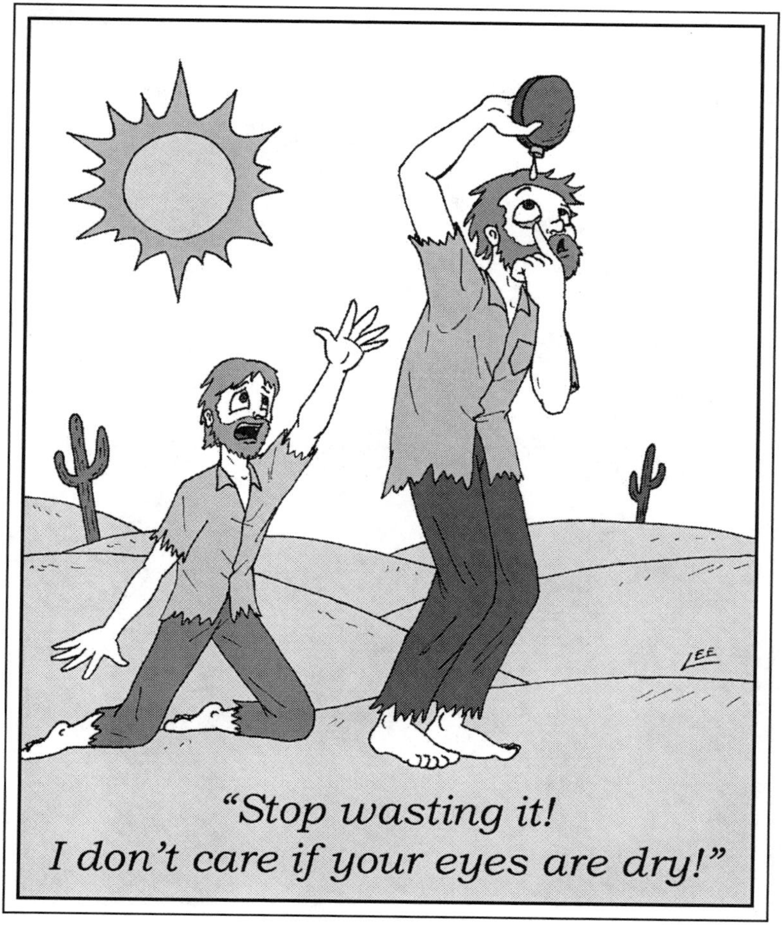
LEE

"Stop wasting it!
I don't care if your eyes are dry!"

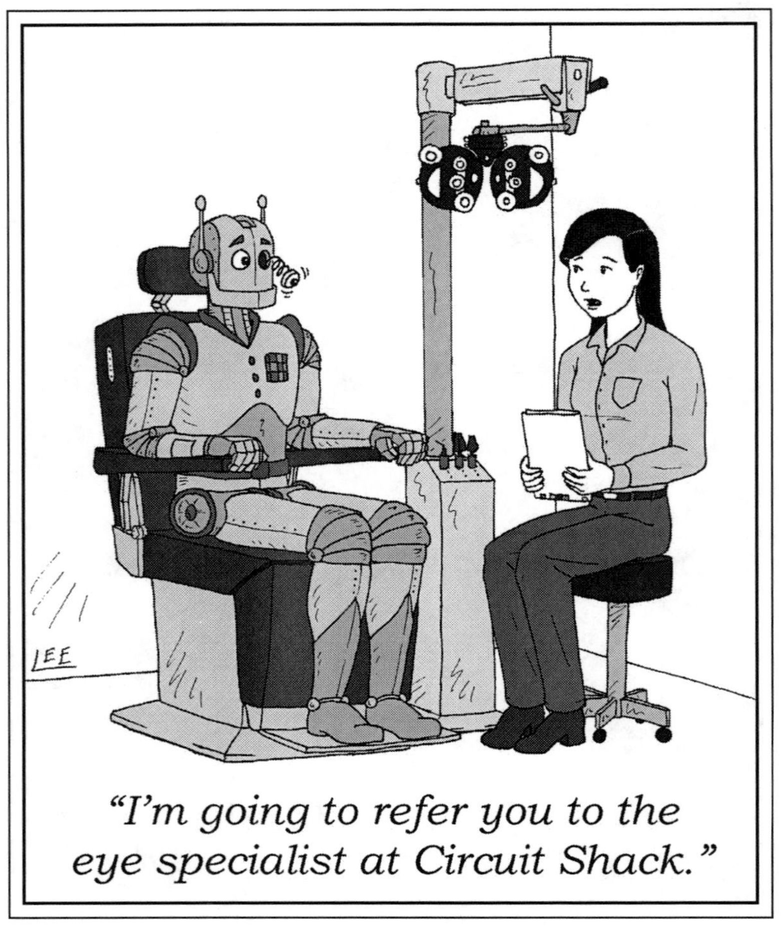
LEE

"I'm going to refer you to the eye specialist at Circuit Shack."

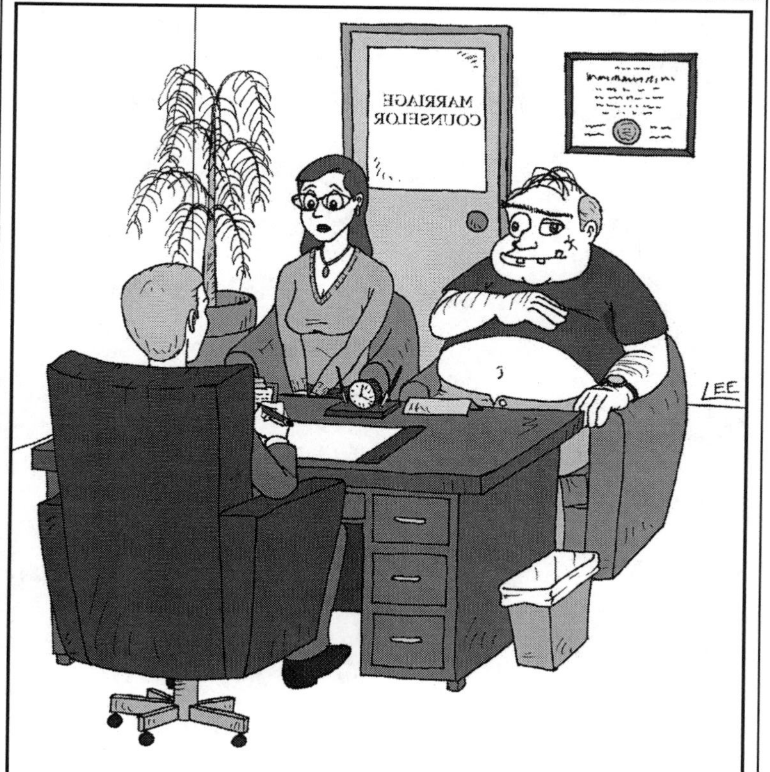
MARRIAGE
COUNSELOR
LEE

"When we met it was love at first sight.
I just wasn't wearing my glasses."

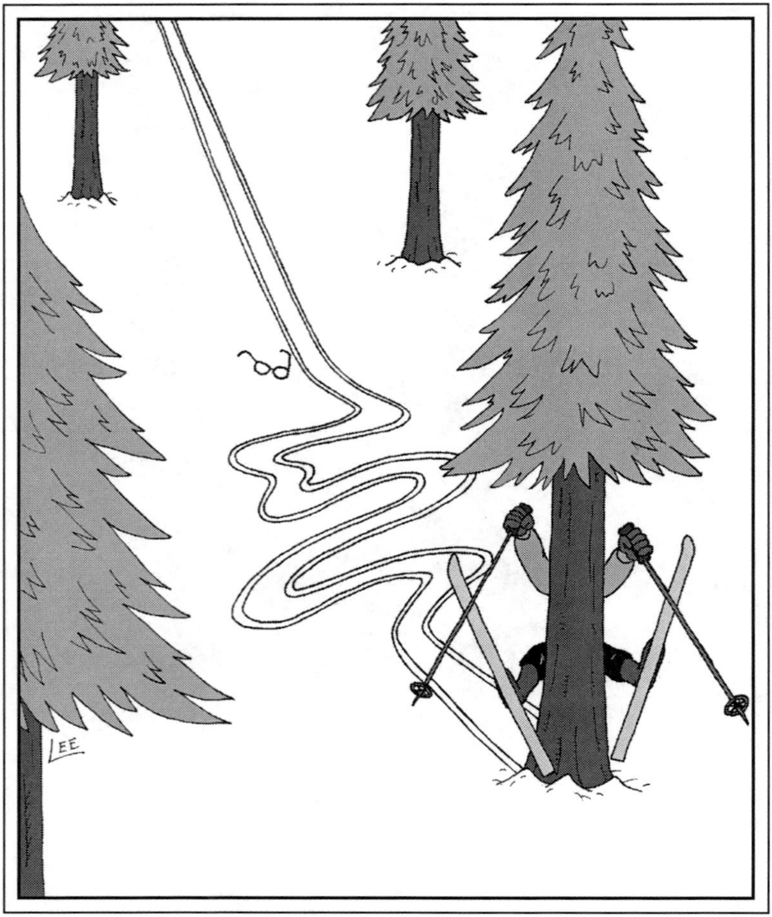
LEE

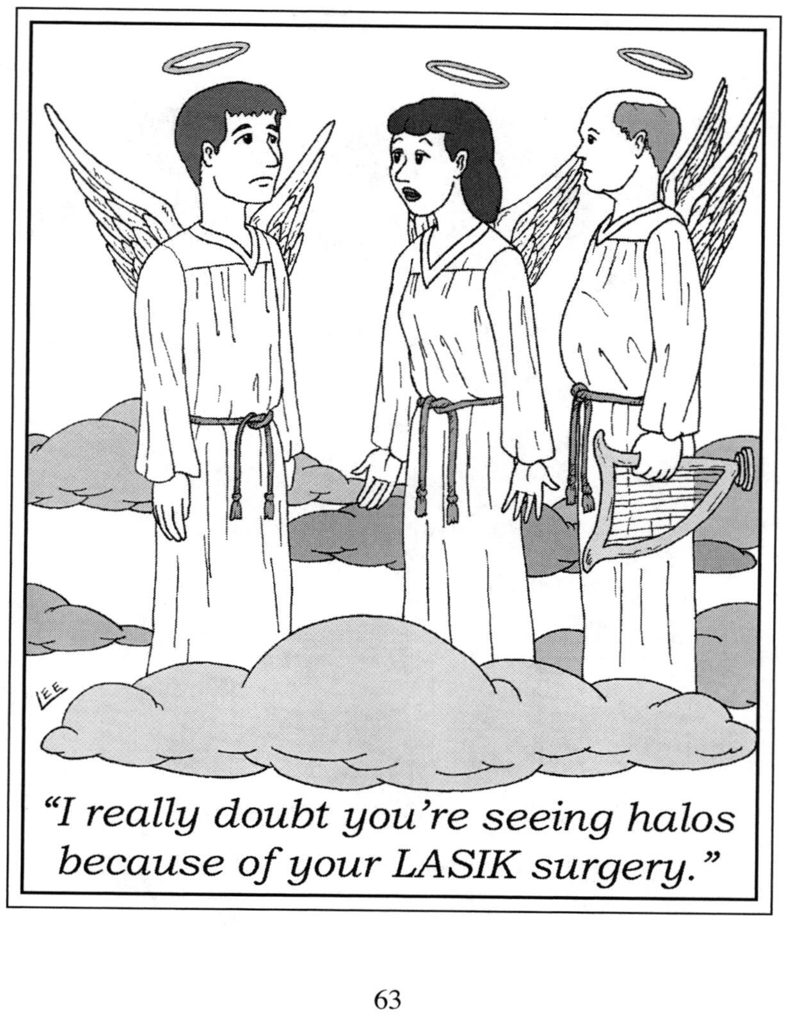
LEE

“I really doubt you’re seeing halos because of your LASIK surgery.”

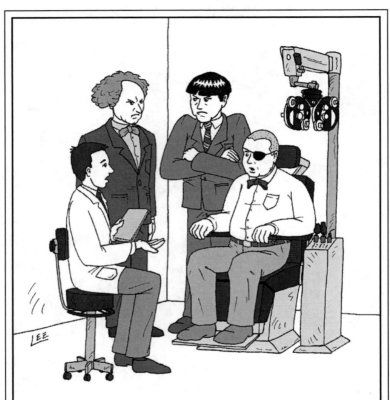

"I'm not saying you can't hit each other... just avoid the eyes."

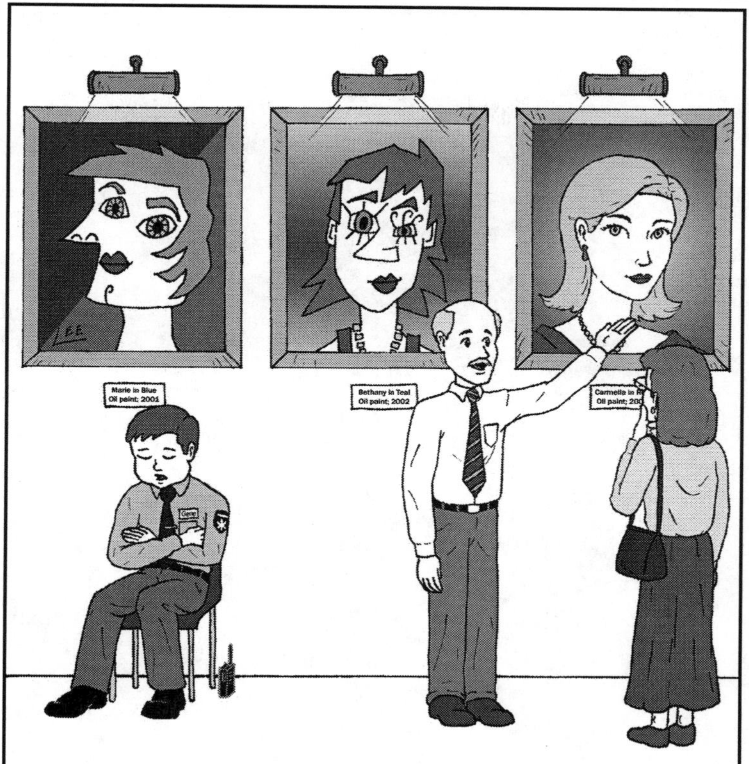
Marie in Blue
Oil paint; 2001
Bethany in Teal
Oil paint; 2002

"...and he painted this piece after finally getting his first eye exam."

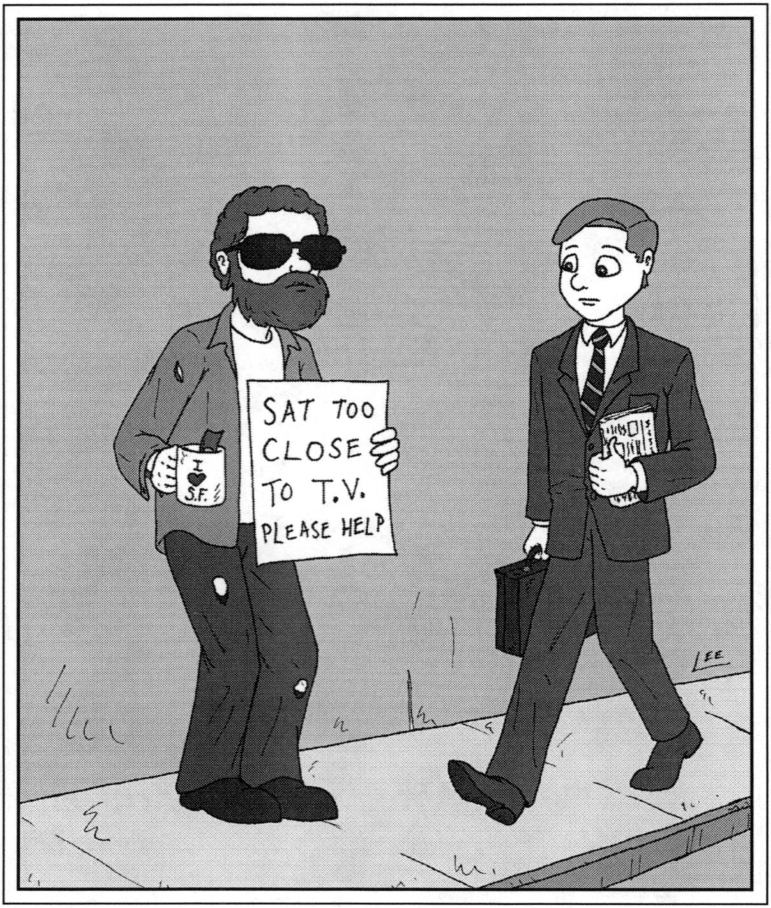
SAT TOO CLOSE TO T.V. PLEASE HELP
I ♥ S.F.
LEE

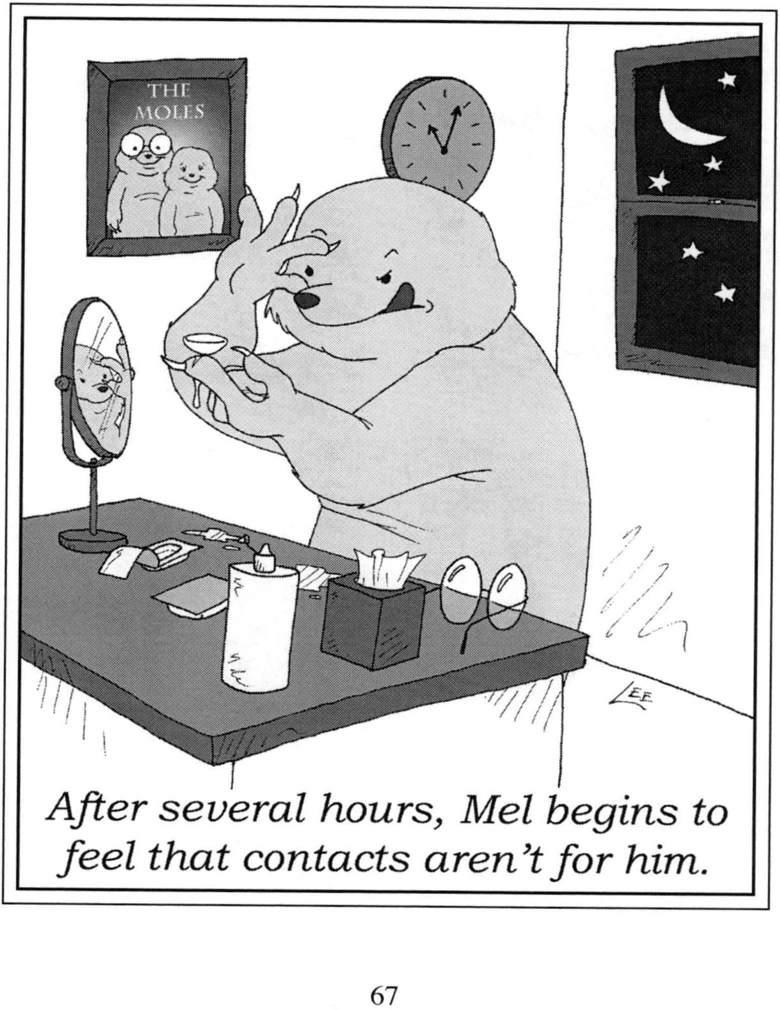
THE
MOLES

After several hours, Mel begins to feel that contacts aren't for him.

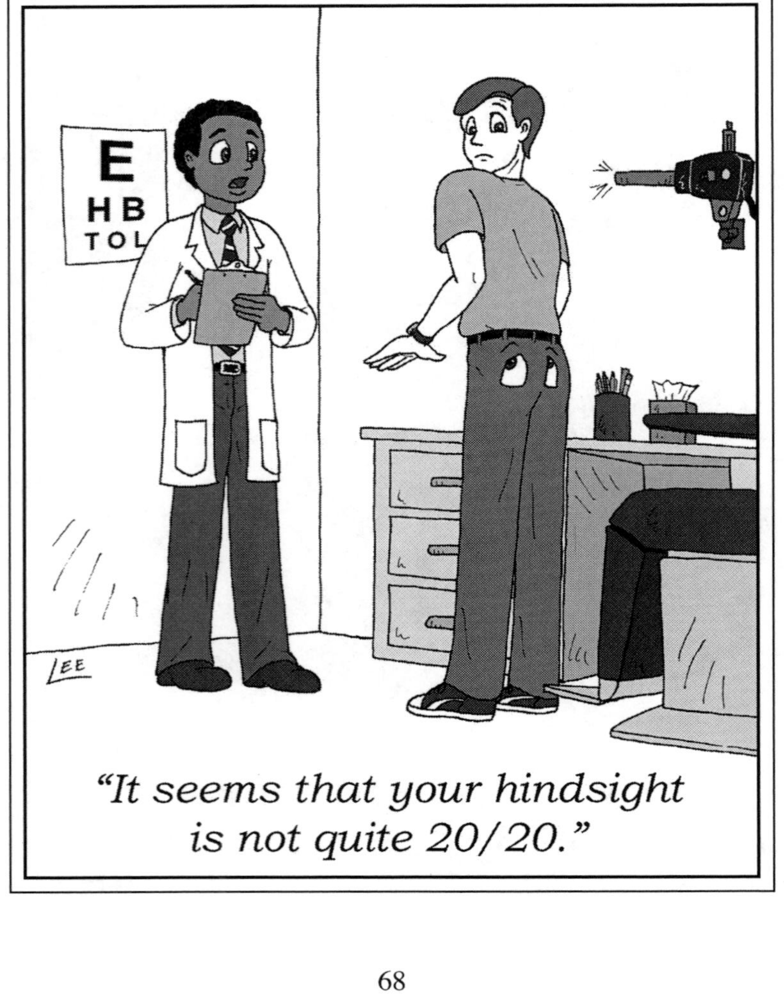
E
HB
TOL
LEE

"It seems that your hindsight is not quite 20/20."

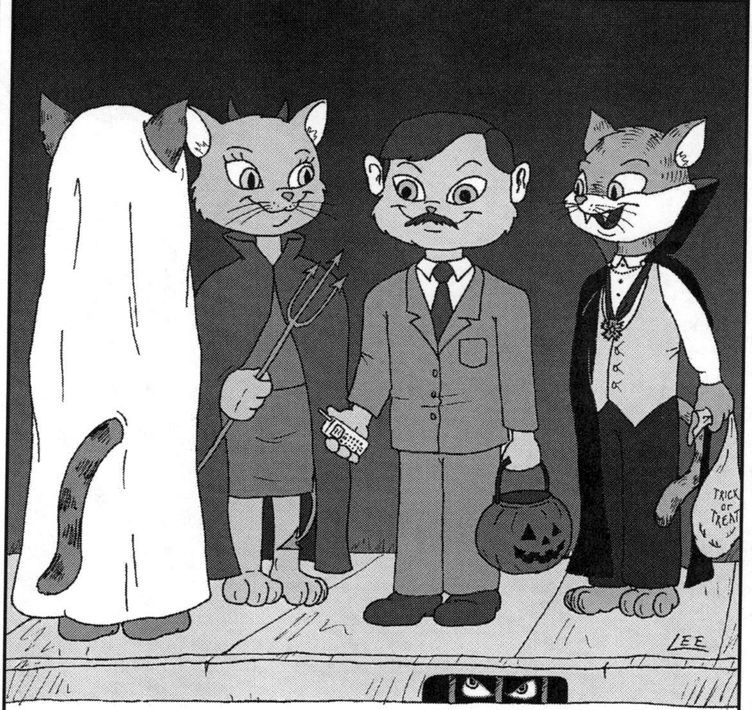
TRICK or TREAT
LEE

"Wow! Those Human Eye contacts really complete the costume!"

I SEE YOUR FOSSIL FRAME AND I'LL RAISE YOU A GUCCI.
TOO RICH FOR ME.
LEE

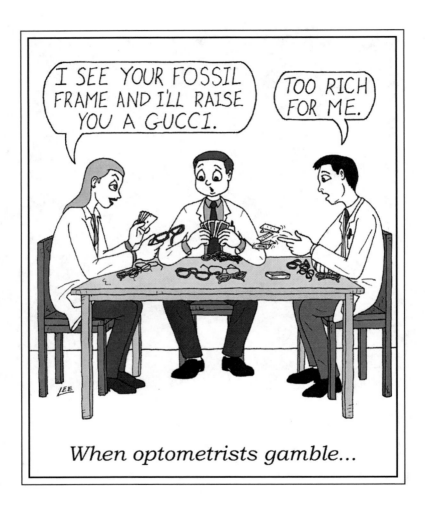

When optometrists gamble...

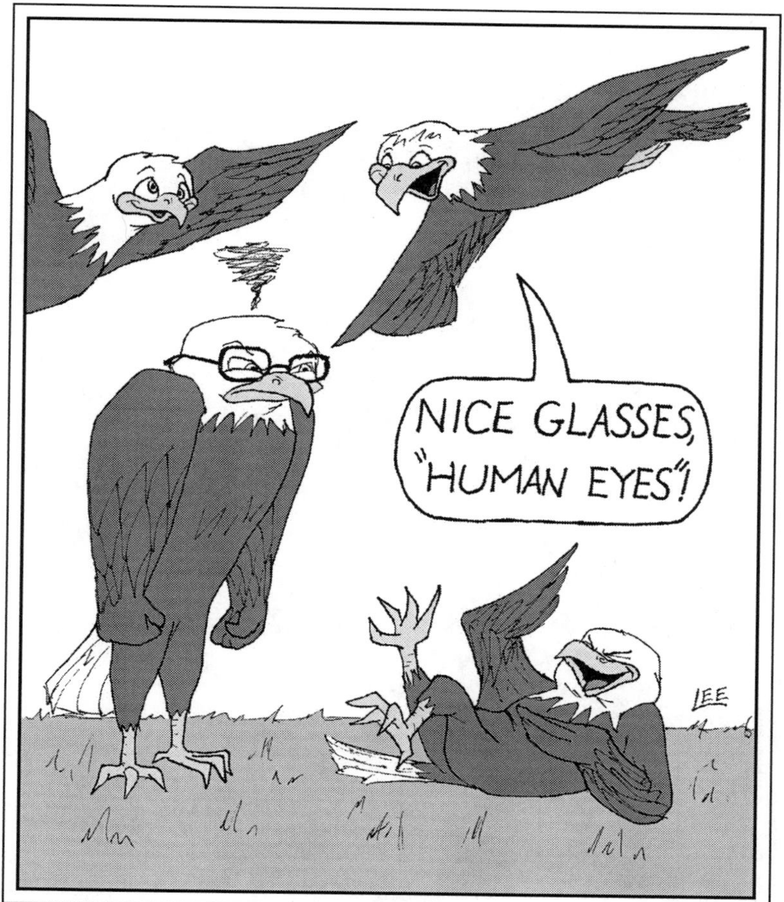
NICE GLASSES, "HUMAN EYES"!
LEE

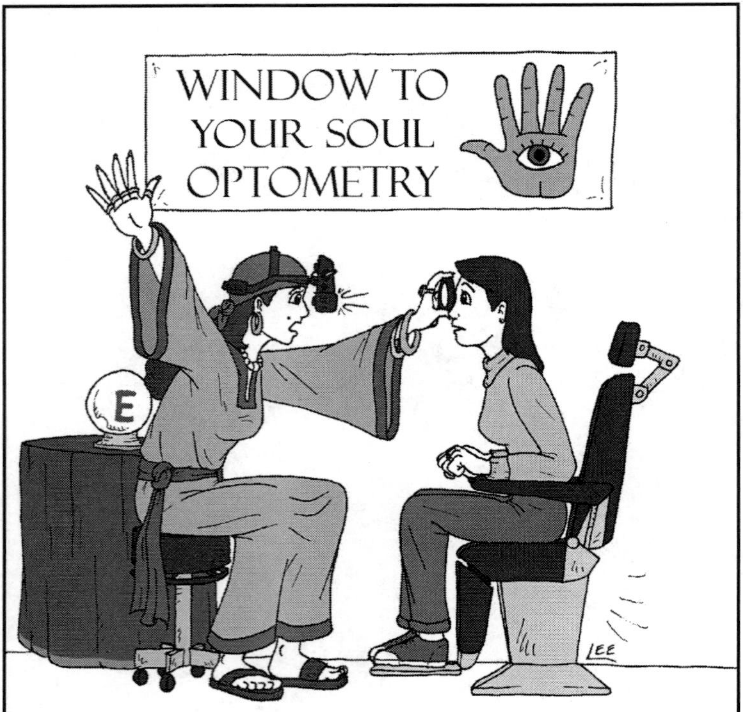
WINDOW TO
YOUR SOUL
OPTOMETRY
E
LEE

"Your retina looks healthy, but your soul looks troubled."

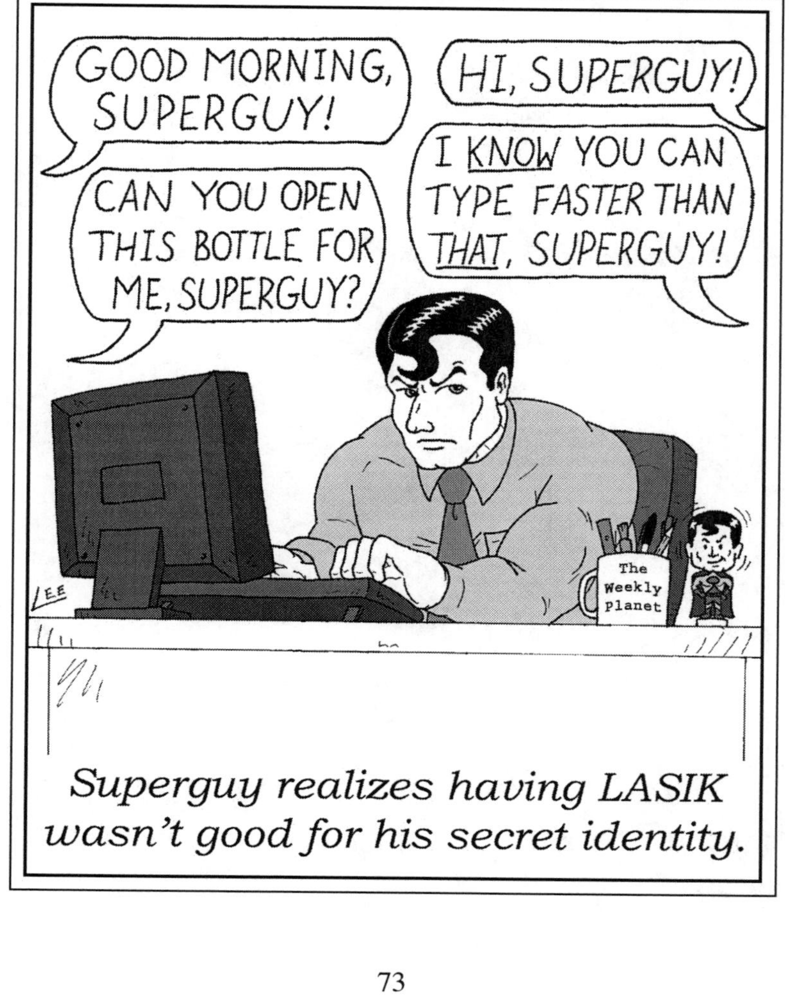
GOOD MORNING, SUPERGUY!
HI, SUPERGUY!
CAN YOU OPEN THIS BOTTLE FOR ME, SUPERGUY?
I KNOW YOU CAN TYPE FASTER THAN THAT, SUPERGUY!
The Weekly Planet
LEE

Superguy realizes having LASIK wasn't good for his secret identity.

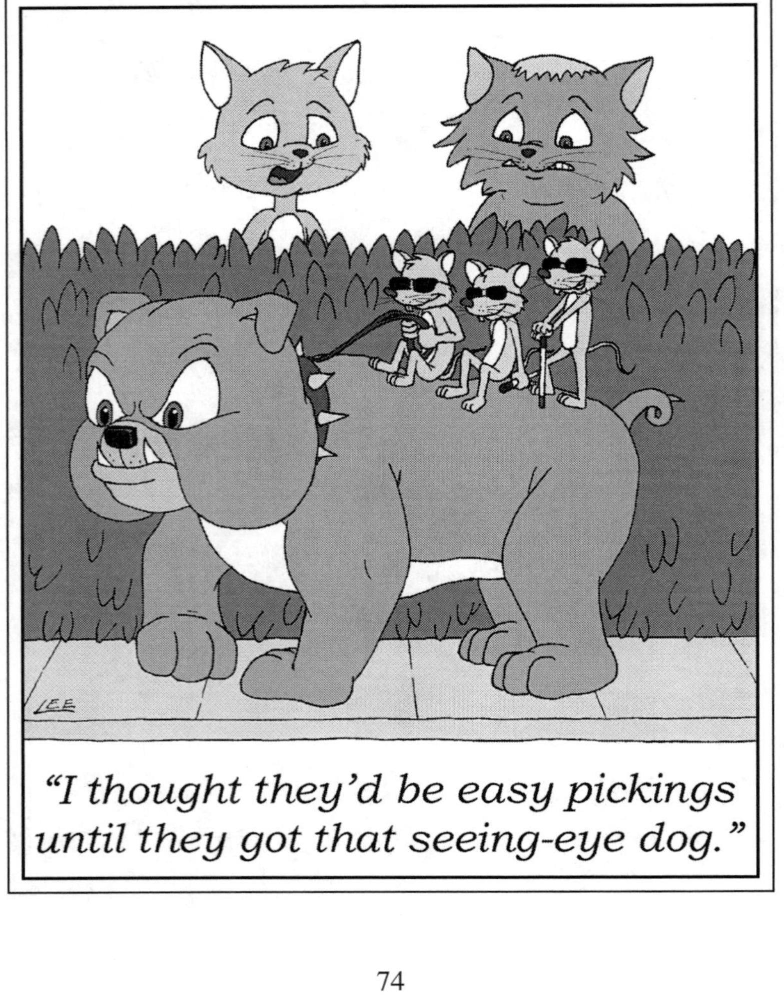
LEE

"I thought they'd be easy pickings until they got that seeing-eye dog."

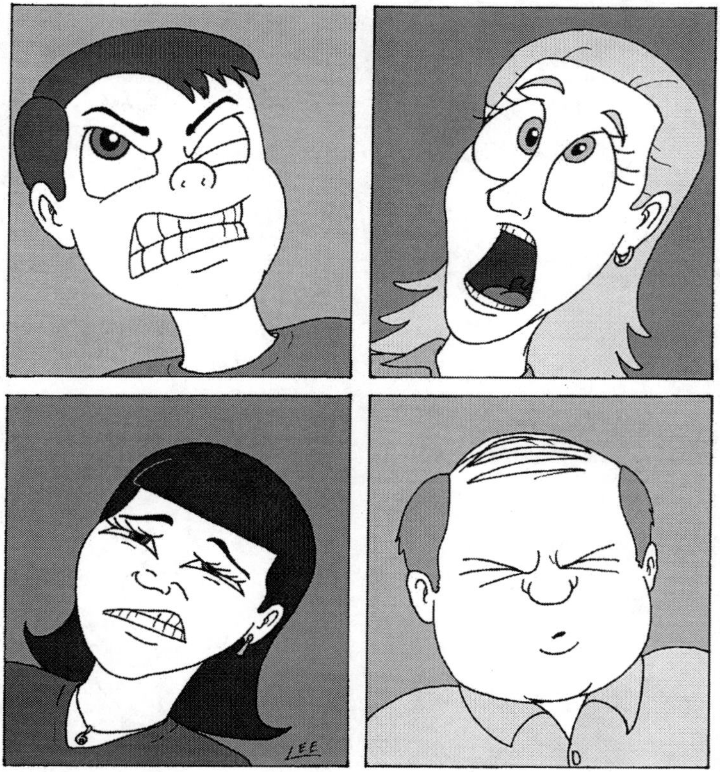
LEE

The Gallery of Eye Drop Faces

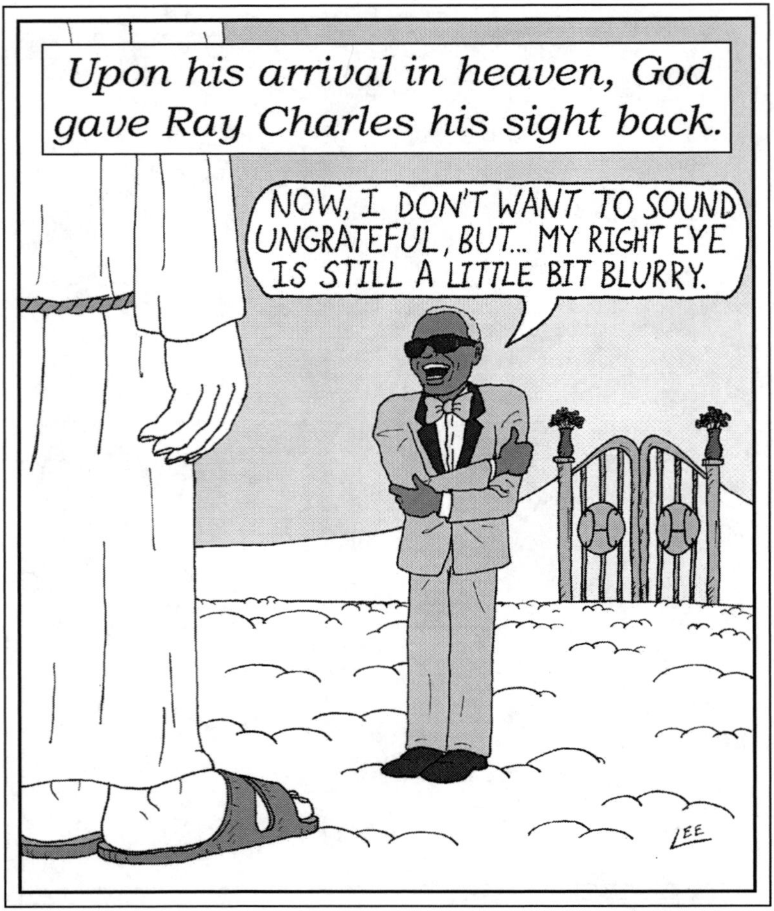
Upon his arrival in heaven, God gave Ray Charles his sight back.
NOW, I DON'T WANT TO SOUND UNGRATEFUL, BUT... MY RIGHT EYE IS STILL A LITTLE BIT BLURRY.
LEE

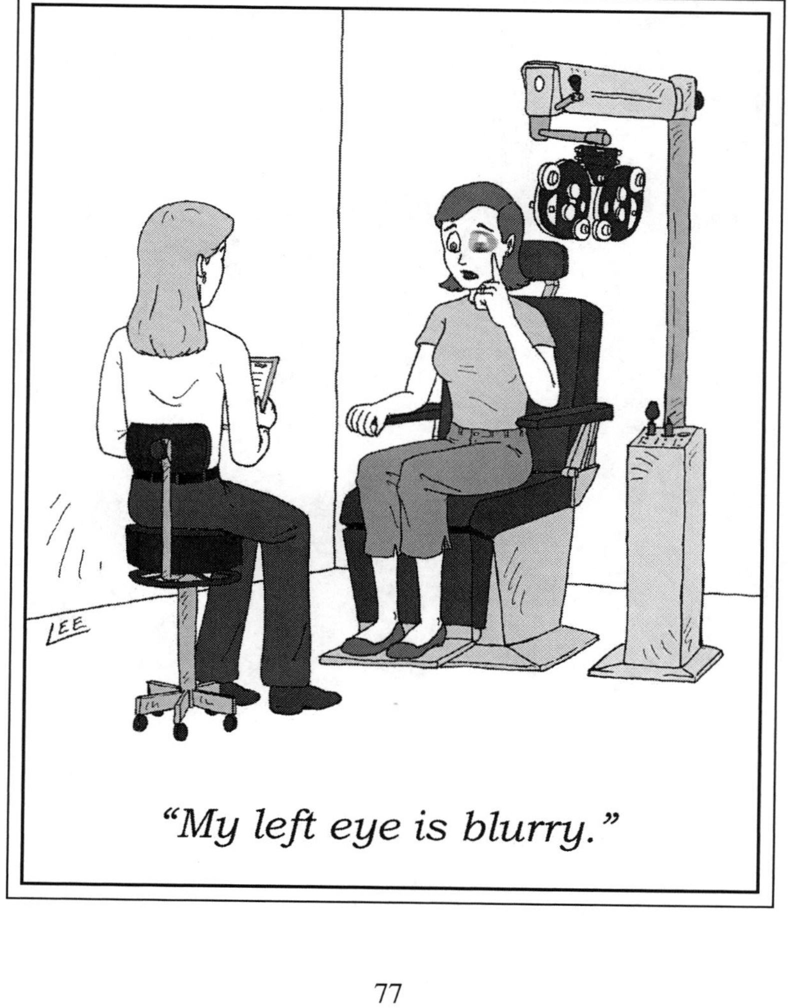
LEE

"My left eye is blurry."

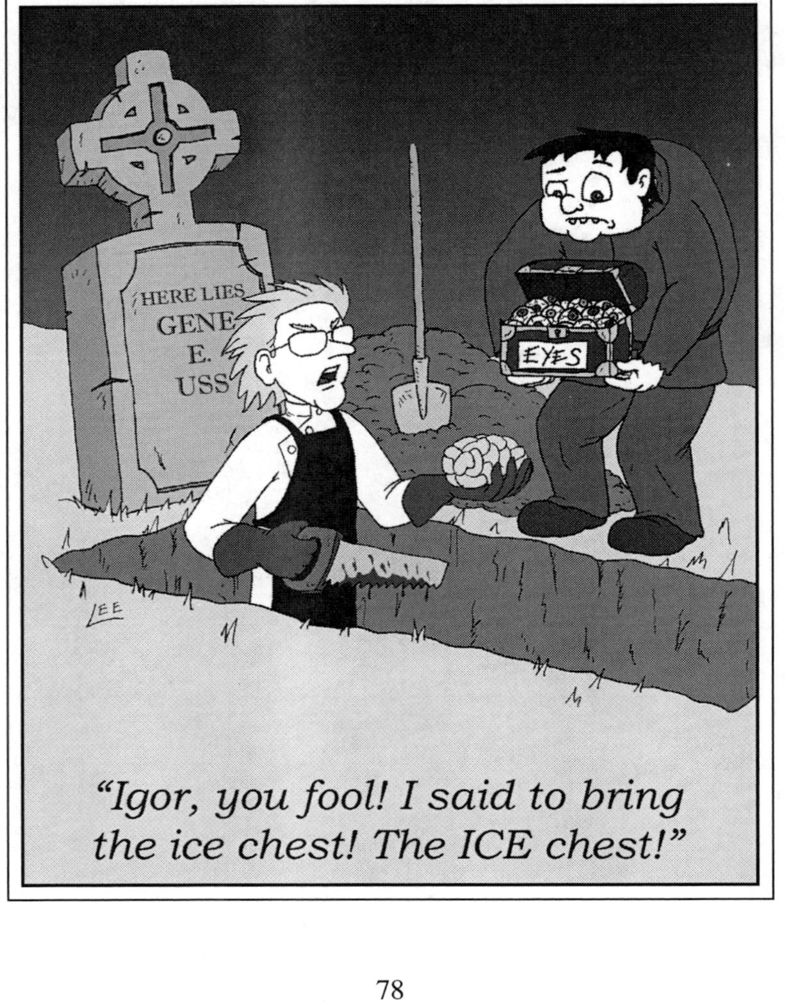
HERE LIES
GENE
E.
USS
EYES
LEE

"Igor, you fool! I said to bring the ice chest! The ICE chest!"

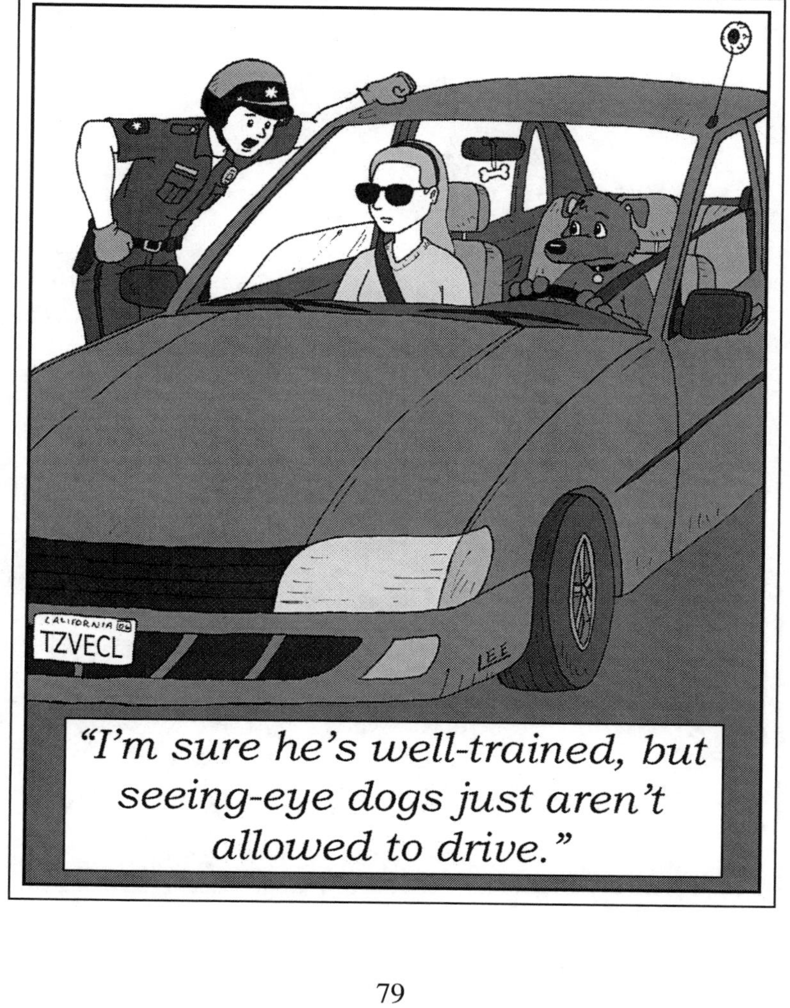
CALIFORNIA
TZVECL
LEE

"I'm sure he's well-trained, but seeing-eye dogs just aren't allowed to drive."

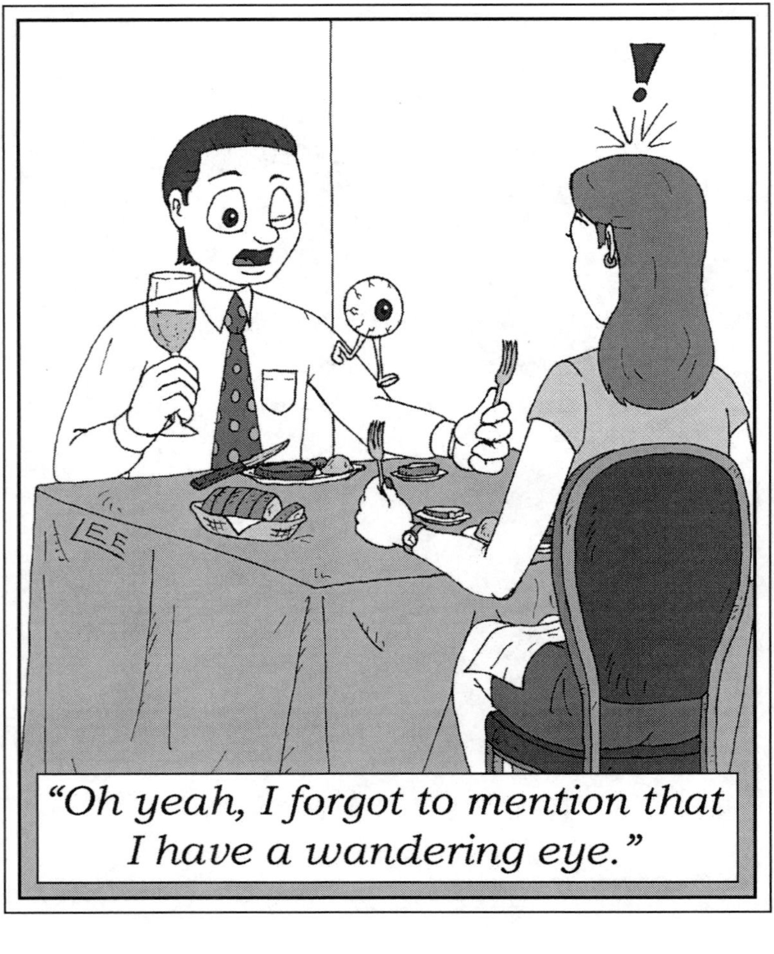
LEE

"Oh yeah, I forgot to mention that I have a wandering eye."

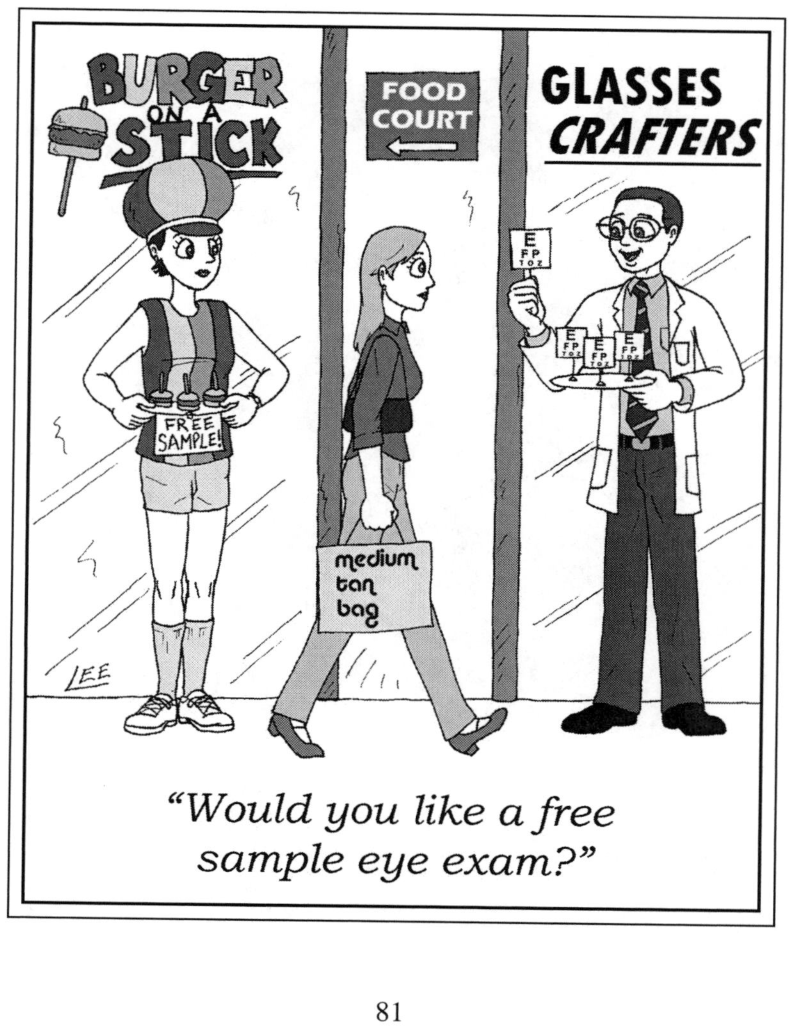
BURGER ON A STICK
FOOD COURT
GLASSES CRAFTERS
FREE SAMPLE!
medium tan bag
LEE

"Would you like a free sample eye exam?"

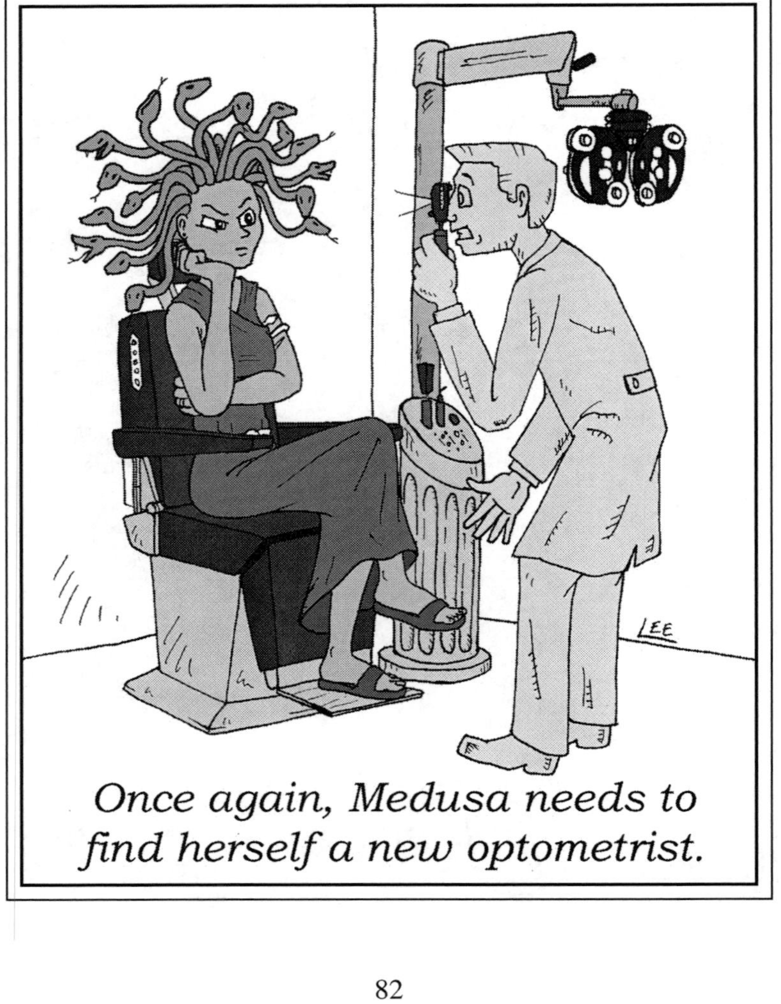
LEE

Once again, Medusa needs to find herself a new optometrist.

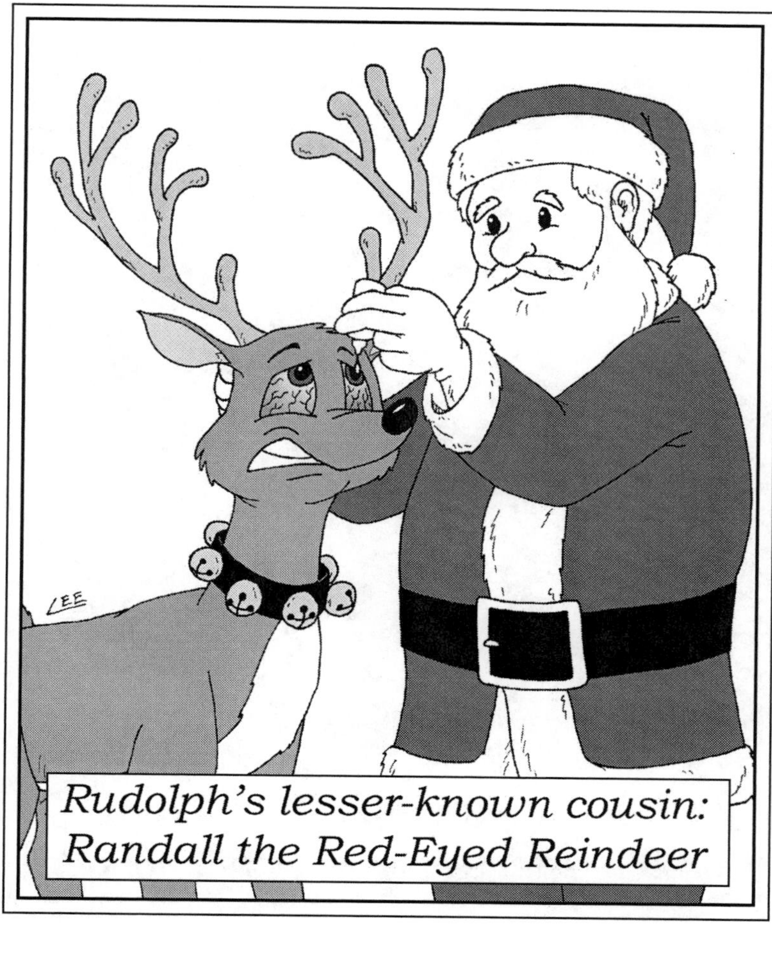
LEE

Rudolph's lesser-known cousin:
Randall the Red-Eyed Reindeer

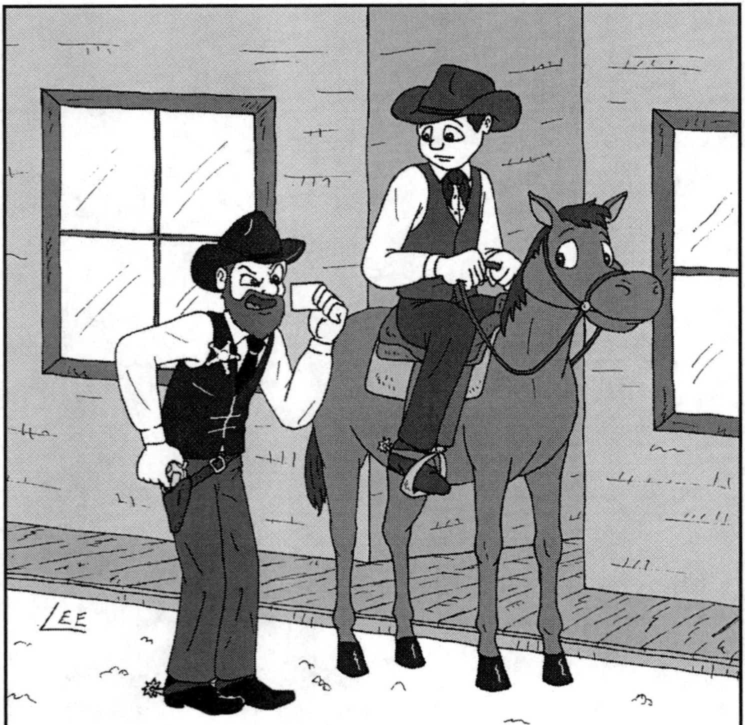
LEE

"Wait just a minute, pardner! Your license says you need to wear corrective lenses to ride this horse!"

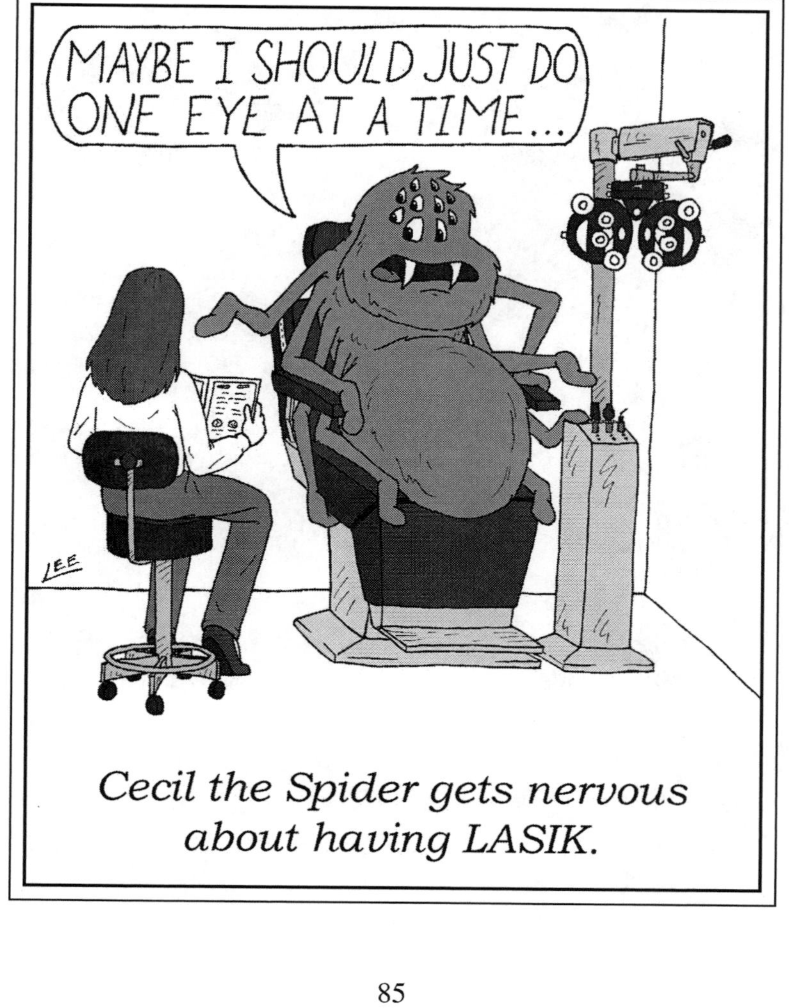
MAYBE I SHOULD JUST DO ONE EYE AT A TIME...
LEE

Cecil the Spider gets nervous about having LASIK.

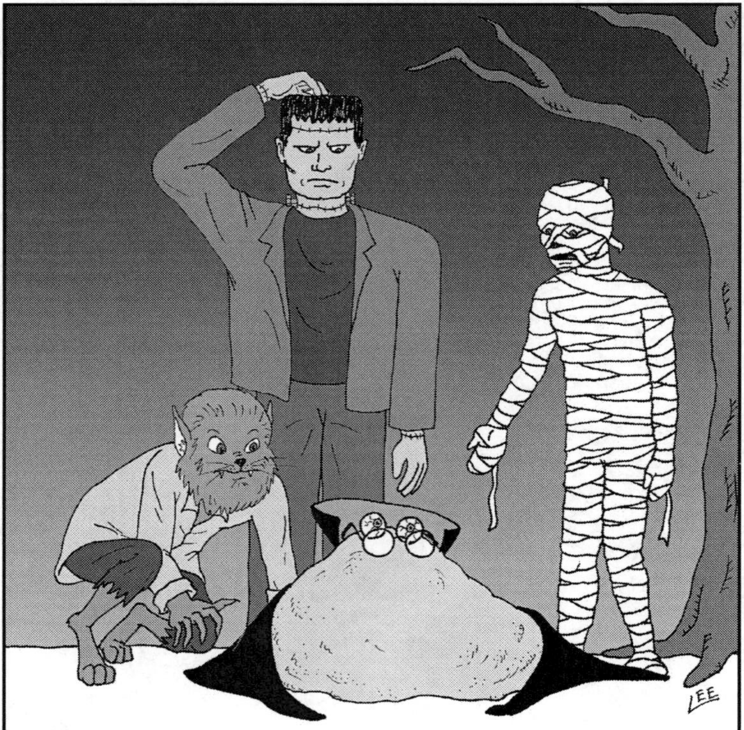
LEE

"His optometrist said his new glasses would protect him from the sun... I guess he just meant his eyes."

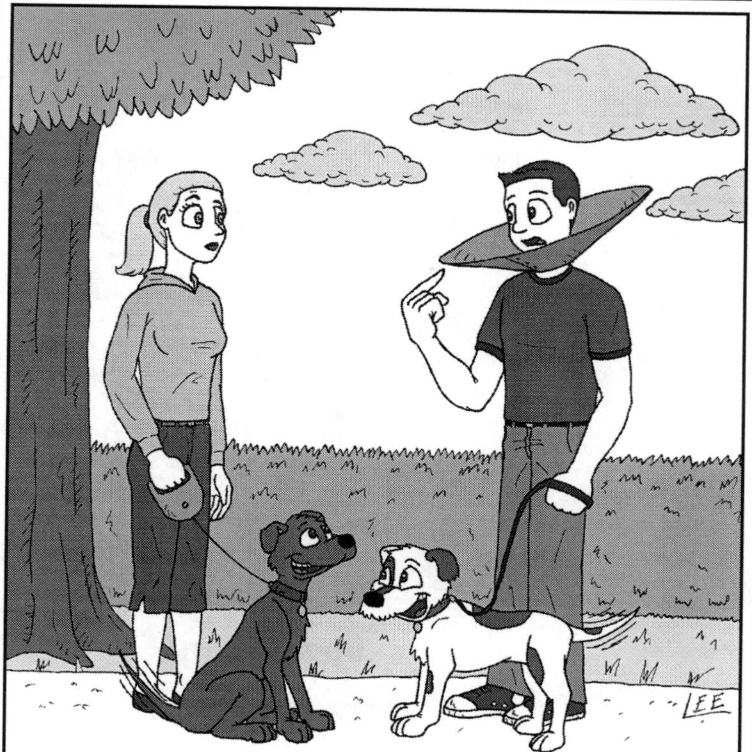
LEE

"My eye doctor told me to wear this so I won't rub my eyes so much."

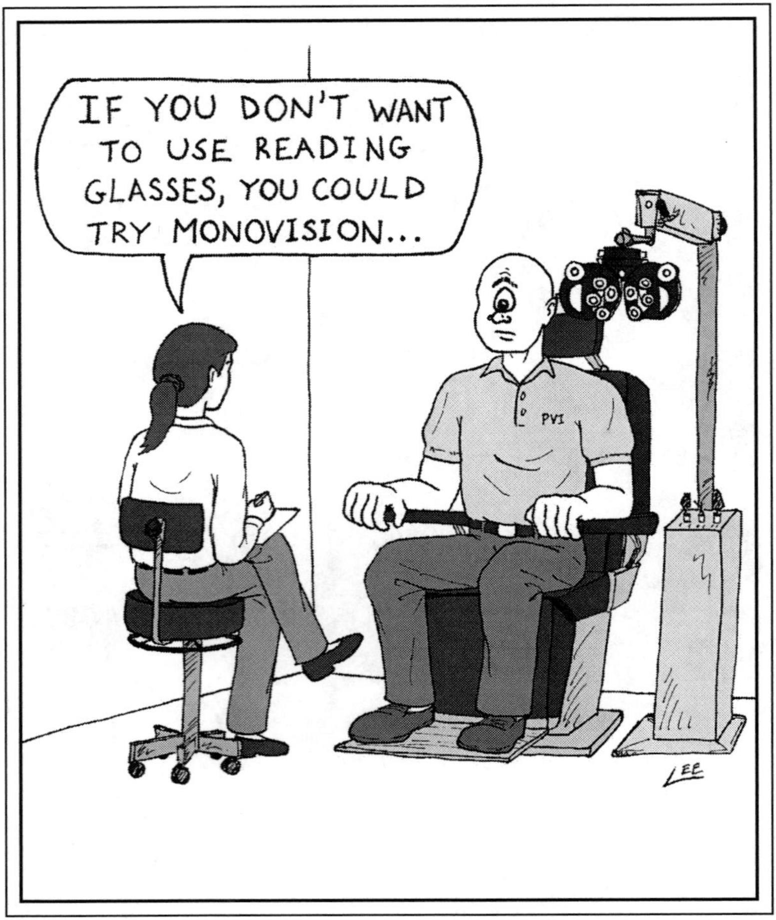
IF YOU DON'T WANT TO USE READING GLASSES, YOU COULD TRY MONOVISION...
PVI
LEE

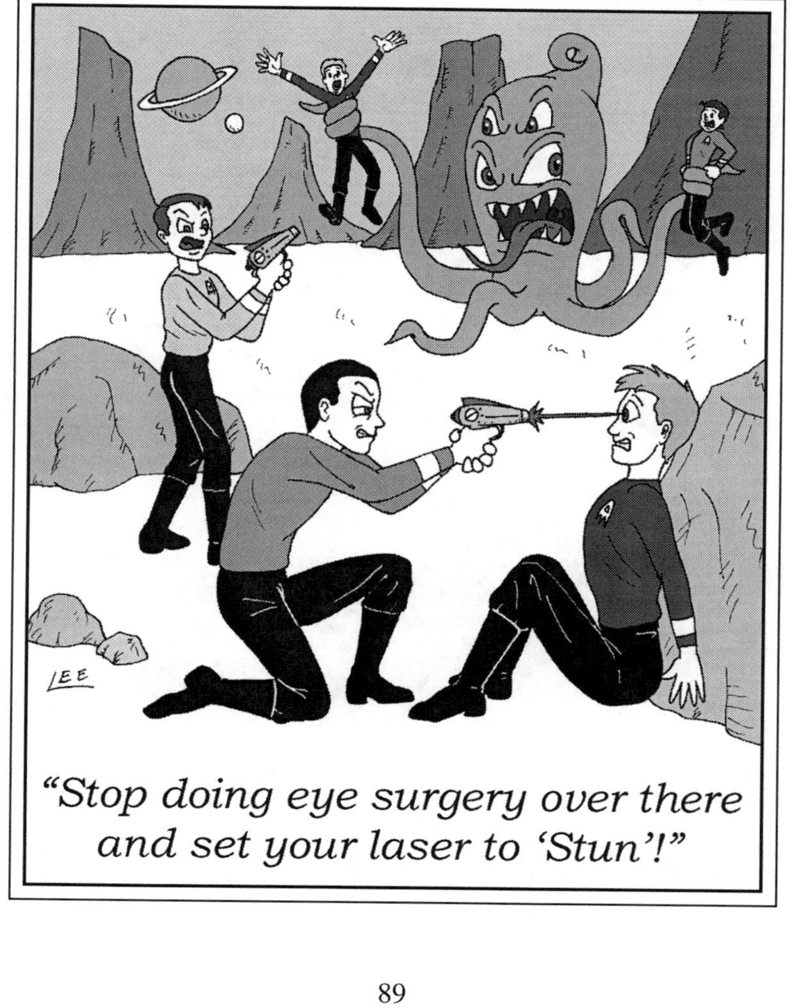
LEE

"Stop doing eye surgery over there and set your laser to 'Stun'!"

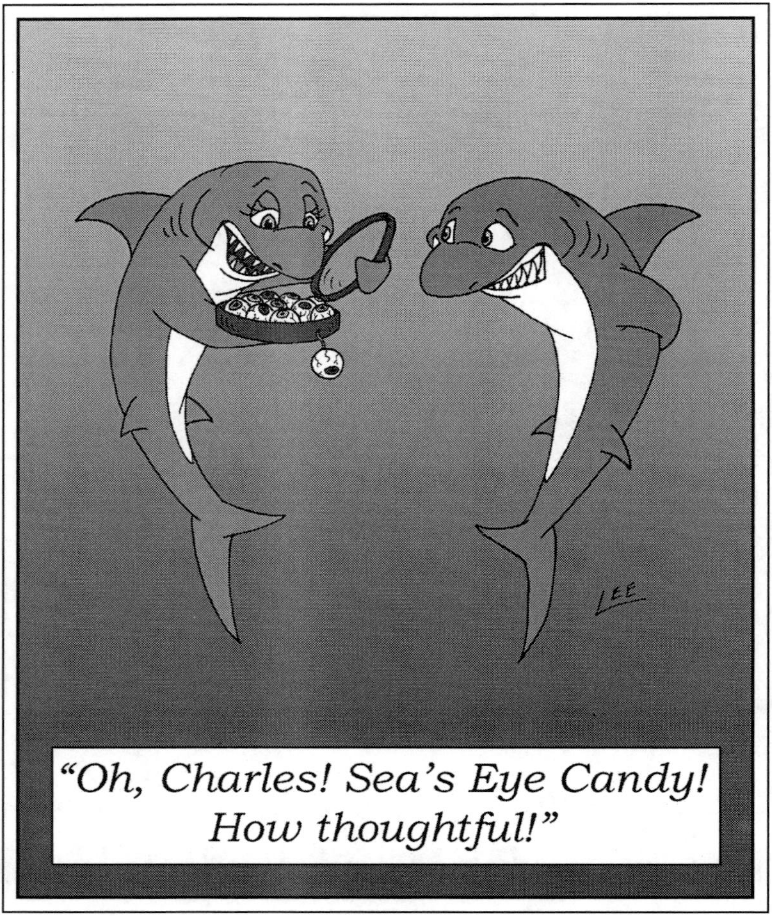
LEE

"Oh, Charles! Sea's Eye Candy! How thoughtful!"

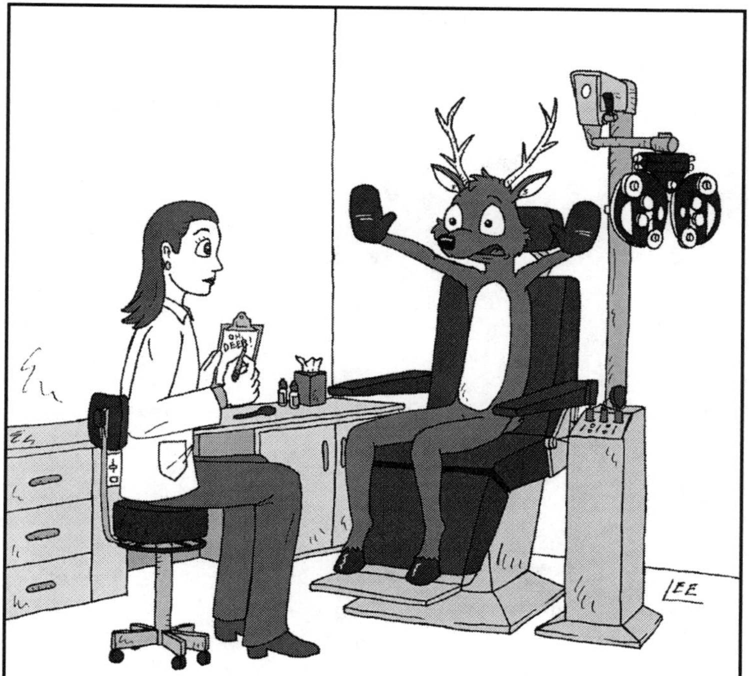
OH DEER!
LEE

"I see a lot of glare and halos around headlights at night and they're so... mesmerizing."

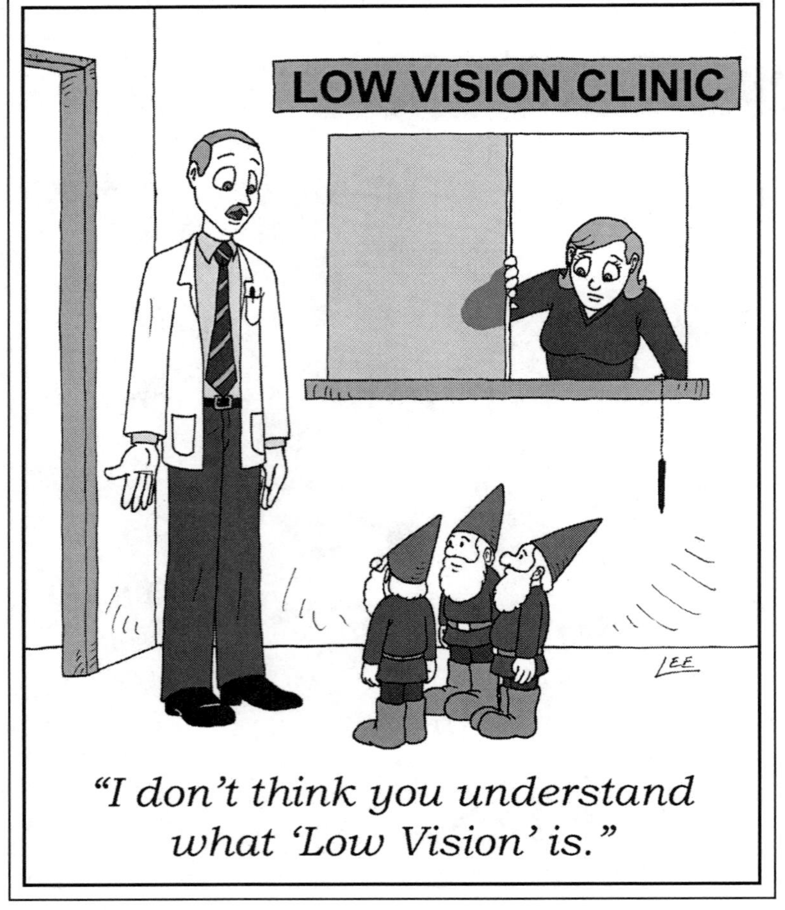
LOW VISION CLINIC
LEE

"I don't think you understand what 'Low Vision' is."

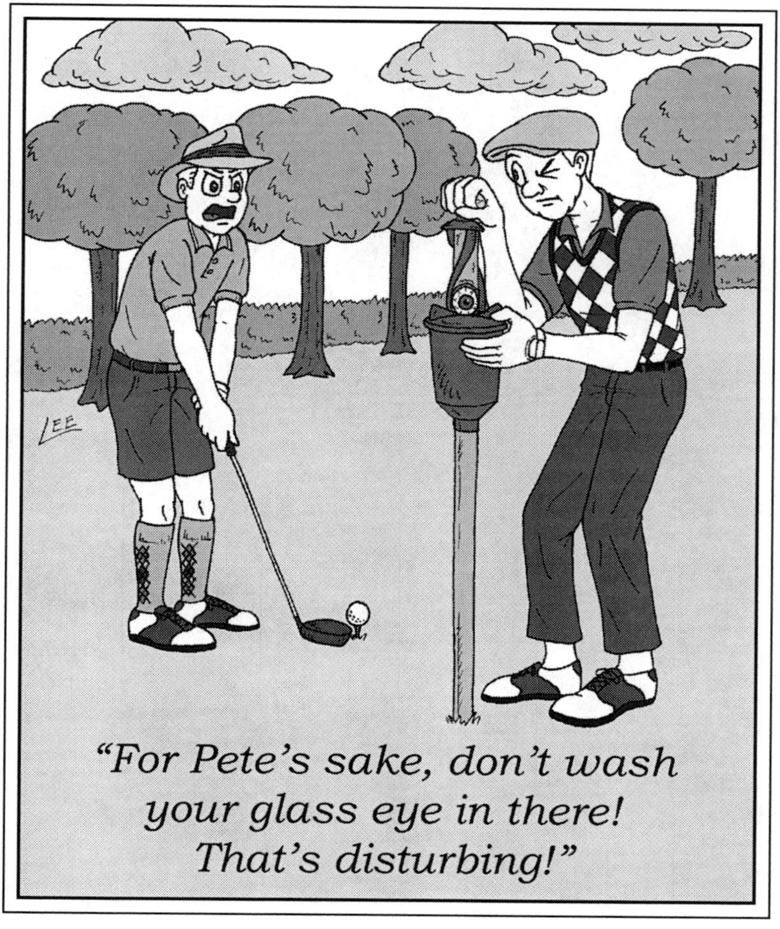
LEE

"For Pete's sake, don't wash your glass eye in there! That's disturbing!"

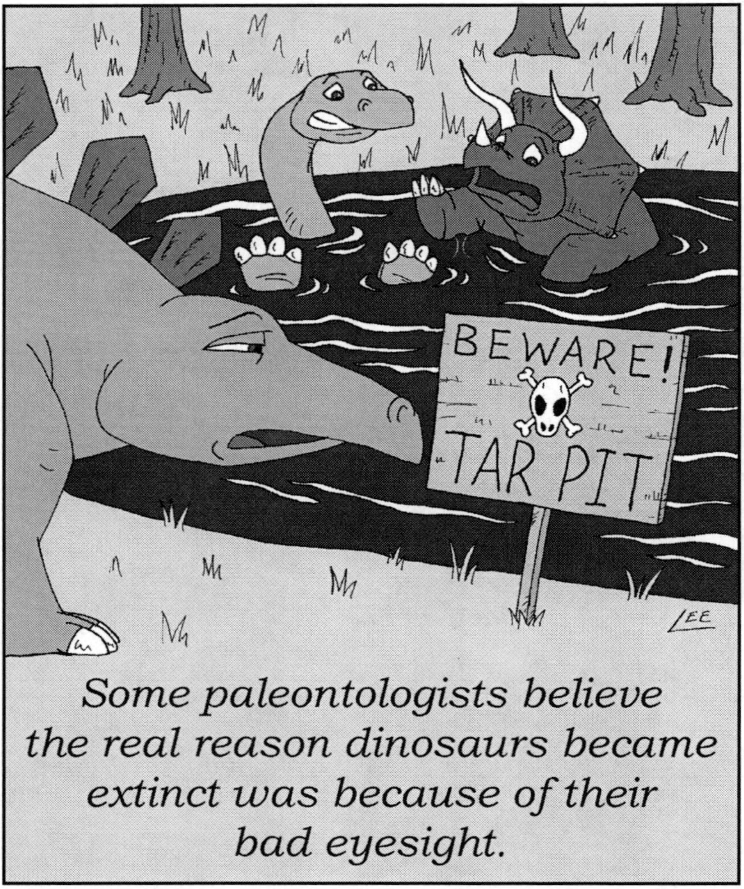
BEWARE!
TAR PIT
LEE

Some paleontologists believe the real reason dinosaurs became extinct was because of their bad eyesight.

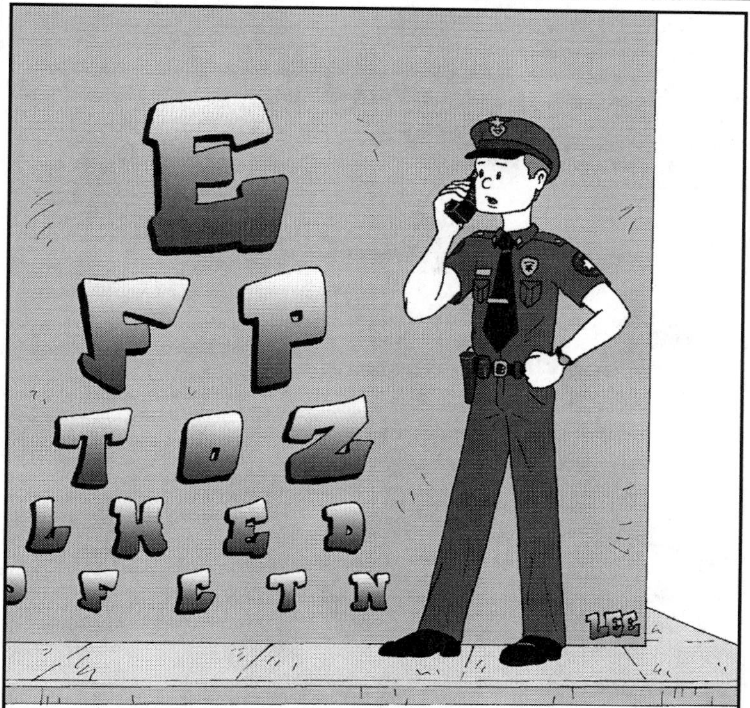
E
F P
T O Z
L K E D
F C T N
LEE

"Be on the lookout. That gang of optometrists is back in town."

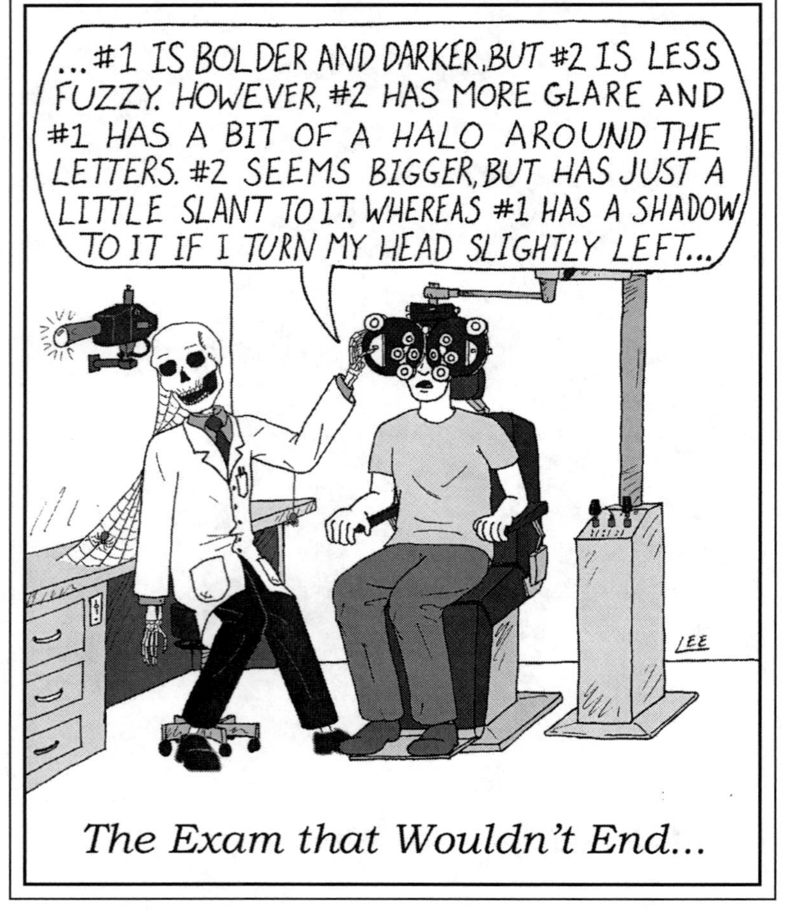
...#1 IS BOLDER AND DARKER, BUT #2 IS LESS FUZZY. HOWEVER, #2 HAS MORE GLARE AND #1 HAS A BIT OF A HALO AROUND THE LETTERS. #2 SEEMS BIGGER, BUT HAS JUST A LITTLE SLANT TO IT. WHEREAS #1 HAS A SHADOW TO IT IF I TURN MY HEAD SLIGHTLY LEFT...
LEE

The Exam that Wouldn't End...

Acknowledgments

There are a few people that helped make this book materialize. First, thank you to my wife, Chrystine, who put up with me the many nights I was engrossed in my cartoons while she sat alone working on a Sudoku puzzle (although, sometimes it felt like she was engrossed in her Sudoku while I sat alone working on my cartoons). Thanks to Cherryl for her great input and ideas. I would also like to acknowledge Gene Faktorovich, Hugh Henry, and Kristin Loke for helping me get the book to print. Finally, a warm thanks to my patients who unwittingly fed me the inspiration to create Sight Gags.

About the Artist

Scott F. Lee, O.D. was born in Hollywood and grew up in South Pasadena, California. He earned his bachelor's degree in Studio Art at the University of California, Irvine while working on the side as a freelance illustrator. After deciding that he enjoyed art more as a hobby than as a job, he attended the University of California, Berkeley, School of Optometry. He graduated in 2002 and has worked in the San Francisco Bay Area ever since.